MW00562309

ANXIETY IN RELATIONSHIPS WORKBOOK

Anxiety in Relationships Workbook

EXERCISES for NURTURING YOURSELF and BUILDING STRONGER RELATIONSHIPS

Sarah Belarde, LCSW

ROCKRIDGE
PRESS

No book, including this one, can ever replace the diagnostic expertise and medical advice of a physician in providing information about your health. The information contained herein is not intended to replace medical advice. You should consult with your doctor before using the information in this or any health-related book.

Copyright © 2022 by Rockridge Press

All rights reserved. No part of this publication may be reproduced, stored in a retrieval system, or transmitted in any form or by any means, electronic, mechanical, photocopying, recording, scanning, or otherwise, without the prior written permission of the Publisher. Requests to the Publisher for permission should be addressed to the Permissions Department, Rockridge Press, 1955 Broadway, Suite 400, Oakland, CA 94612.

First Rockridge Press trade paperback edition 2022

Rockridge Press and the Rockridge Press logo are trademarks or registered trademarks of Callisto Media Inc. and/or its affiliates in the United States and other countries and may not be used without written permission.

For general information on our other products and services, please contact our Customer Care Department within the United States at (866) 744-2665, or outside the United States at (510) 253-0500.

Paperback ISBN: 978-1-68539-461-5 | eBook ISBN: 978-1-68539-975-7

Manufactured in the United States of America

Art Director: Helen Bruno
Interior and Cover Designer: Amanda Kirk
Art Producer: Samantha Ulban
Editor: Adrian Potts
Production Manager: Holly Haydash

10 9 8 7 6 5 4 3 2 1 0

Contents

Introduction

In the United States, nearly one in five adults has an anxiety disorder that causes them to have worries and fears about the future. Most adults will have a romantic relationship during the course of their life, and developing anxiety about relationships is exceedingly common.

Whether you are in a serious relationship, casually dating, or hoping to date in the future, chances are you have had an anxious thought about romance. People worry about getting into relationships, ending up alone, whether they picked the right partner, or whether they are good enough all the time. These frequent worries can truly impact our behavior and can lead to avoidance, isolation, sadness, and anxiety. Relationships can be hard, and our anxious thoughts about our partners, dating, and your future can make them harder. You are not alone in feeling this type of anxiety.

Most adults experience relationship anxiety at some point in their life, and many are able to seek help and learn strategies to manage their anxious thoughts in order to go on and have healthy relationships. No matter what stage you are at in your relationship journey, this workbook is designed to help you address your anxiety, where it comes from, and how to manage it.

I personally have dealt with anxiety throughout my life, and this is what drew me to the field of mental health. As a therapist, I am surrounded by information and skills I have learned and studied throughout the years to help not only my clients but also myself. Specifically, relationship anxiety is something that has interested me because most adults are affected by it, and it is something that can be addressed.

Many times in my practice a client will come to me feeling hopeless about worries involving their relationship or dating, and with practice, processing, and hard work they develop a deep understanding of where their anxiety comes from and how to manage it. As a result, they go on to foster healthy relationships. You can also heal from your relationship anxiety. This workbook consists of a compilation of strategies my clients and I have found useful throughout my nine years as a mental health therapist.

This workbook is a great starting point to begin to manage your relationship anxiety, as well as a fantastic supplement to therapy. While this is a tool to begin healing from relationship anxiety, it is also important to note that it is not a replacement for therapy, medication, or medical treatment. Don't hesitate to reach out to resources outside this book if you are experiencing any debilitating feelings of depression or anxiety.

In this workbook, I will ask you to reflect on healthy and unhealthy tendencies in your relationships, which sometimes brings up strong feelings. If you are a victim of domestic violence or abuse—or if you become worried about the health of your relationship throughout the course of this workbook—please seek assistance from a therapist or other resources. There is no shame in seeking help or treatment.

I want to offer you praise for taking steps to alleviate some of the relationship anxiety in your life. What an incredible step this is! My hope is that as you progress throughout this workbook you will continue to use the skills you learn and begin to feel less and less relationship anxiety.

How to Use This Book

This workbook will encourage you to engage with the teachings in each chapter. This book is broken up into two parts. In part 1, you will be introduced to relationship anxiety, learn how to understand your anxieties, and figure out how self-discovery can be an important tool in dealing with relationship anxiety. Part 2 dives into how to address your relationship anxiety and provides exercises to complete in the book, prompts to explore feelings, practices to continue your work outside this book, and affirmations to provide validation and encouragement.

Each chapter builds on the previous one, so it is important to complete it in order. The goal of this workbook is to serve as a resource that you can continue to come back to once completed. With that in mind, feel free to highlight exercises that are most helpful along the way.

PART ONE

An Introduction to Anxiety in Relationships

YOU MAY BE IN A RELATIONSHIP WITH A GREAT PERSON YOU love. They are kind, respectful, and communicative, but you find yourself constantly questioning yourself, your partner, and the relationship. You can't seem to stop wondering, *Will this last? Am I settling? Are they hiding something?* These constant worries may be a sign that you are experiencing relationship anxiety.

Relationship anxiety refers to feelings of worry, insecurity, and doubt that appear even when things are going well. It is also possible to feel this type of anxiety when you are not in a serious relationship. In fact, it can cause issues for you when dating or even just thinking about future relationships.

In part 1 of this workbook, we will focus on understanding relationship anxiety, how to identify it, where it comes from, and what triggers it. We will also review strategies to assist you in managing this anxiety, building coping skills, and identifying how self-discovery and reflection can benefit you in this process.

If you believe you have relationship anxiety, don't panic. The fact that you have started this workbook is a powerful indicator of your willingness to reflect on yourself and learn strategies to cope and heal. It is absolutely possible to feel more safe and secure in yourself and your relationship.

CHAPTER ONE

Understanding Your Anxieties

IN MY PRACTICE AS A MENTAL HEALTH THERAPIST, AS WELL AS in my personal life, I have seen how deeply anxiety can impact relationships. Anxiety can be defined as a persistent worry, fear, or sense of uneasiness that is difficult to control regarding an everyday situation. It is common to feel anxiety in a romantic relationship. Whether your relationship anxiety comes from a lack of reassurance, worries about finding a partner, or doubts about the future, it is important to acknowledge and address the issues. Understanding your anxiety and worries about building a healthy relationship is the first step to making a change toward being your best self.

Anxiety in relationships can be complex, and this workbook is designed to help you sort through your feelings. In this chapter we will discuss where your anxiety comes from, how past relationships can impact anxiety in your current relationship, and behaviors and actions that may be signs of relationship anxiety. Most important, I want to validate that anxiety is a typical piece of relationships, and it is something you can work through. Acknowledging the anxiety, seeking help, and understanding your triggers is a powerful first step on a journey to healing.

CASE STUDY | **Francisco**

Francisco has recently taken a position where he works from home. His wife, Carmen, goes into the office for work. It is a busy season for her, and she has been working longer hours, often missing dinner and checking in with him less throughout the day. Francisco starts to wonder if his wife is still interested in him. He worries that they've grown apart and he isn't doing enough since beginning to work at home. He wants to talk to her about it but doesn't know what to say and fears that she will think he's overreacting. He has started to go to bed earlier to avoid conversations when she gets home. He also notices he is having shortness of breath, feels restless throughout the day, and that he can't stop thinking that his marriage is failing. His worst fear is winding up divorced like his parents.

Over the weekend, his wife asks him what has been wrong lately and says she feels like he's avoiding her. Francisco finally opens up to her about some of his worries and explains that he fears that they are growing apart. Carmen shares that she does not feel this way and that she is just overwhelmed at work. Carmen suggests that Francisco may be experiencing anxiety issues that are affecting their relationship. After doing some research on relationship anxiety, Francisco feels relief and begins to look into how to work through his feelings.

What Is Anxiety in Relationships?

Anxiety has been around for all of human existence. It evolved as a fear response to possible danger, like being eaten by an animal, helping our ancestors confront or flee perceived threats. During these times, staying vigilant to our surroundings helped people stay alive. While we no longer face the same immediate threats to our safety today, our brains are still equipped with the same survival mechanisms, which can lead to excessive worry about other things in our daily lives, including our relationships.

Whether you are starting to date or in a more serious partnership, you have probably felt relationship anxiety at some point. We have all heard about the beginning stages of a relationship when you or a friend are waiting for a person of interest to call you or text you back, and your thoughts begin to head for the worst. Some of those negative thoughts can include, *They must not like me anymore, I must have said something stupid,* or *Maybe it's about how I look?* If you have anxiety in your everyday life, it is very common for it to transfer over to your relationships. People with general anxiety or social anxiety often worry about how others judge them or have a fear of rejection. The vulnerability that comes with romantic relationships may cause that anxiety to build.

Anxiety in relationships consists of worries, repetitive thoughts, and fears you have about your union. It can cause stress for both partners and, if not addressed, can lead to certain hardships. In a psychological study, researchers assessed married couples where one partner was anxious and the other was not. The research found that the degree of daily distress reported by the unanxious partner was significantly associated with the anxious partner's level of anxiety on that particular day. The same study also concluded that anxious couples who displayed communication and support with each other reported higher levels of relationship satisfaction, which assisted in minimizing anxiety. While relationship anxiety is something serious, it is also something that can be alleviated with support and open communication with your partner.

Common Symptoms of Relationship Anxiety

Pursuing a romantic relationship can feel overwhelming. In dating and relationships, we often don't know what the outcome will be, and there can be many unknowns. *Will they like me? Will we end up together? Am I settling?* These worries often create an increased anxious response with our partners. Anxiety in relationships manifests differently for each person, and symptoms affect people mentally, emotionally, and physically. Some of the more common manifestations of relationship anxiety include physical restlessness and fatigue, emotional desire for control, and negative thinking leading to avoidance and sabotage.

Symptoms of this type of anxiety can be difficult to identify if you have a history of general anxiety. When anxious thoughts become a typical part of your daily experience, recognizing them becomes more of a challenge. The following sections will assist you in assessing if you have developed relationship anxiety. It can be helpful to begin by taking time to think about if you have worries about your relationship and reflect on how they impact you mentally, emotionally, or physically.

Mental Symptoms

A core component of addressing anxiety is assessing our thoughts and how they affect our feelings and behaviors. When we feel anxious, it is common for our thoughts to be more negative, often thinking of the worst-case scenario or the glass being half empty. These adverse thoughts can cause us to feel sadness and higher levels of anxiety. In relationship anxiety, they can create a pattern of avoidance and isolation leading to concentration issues, difficulty sleeping, distraction, and irritability. If you are noticing these mental symptoms, it is important to further explore how relationship anxiety is affecting you.

Emotional Symptoms

Relationship anxiety impacts individuals on a deep emotional level. Panic, fear, and worry are symptoms that many people with anxiety experience. In relationships, this looks like overwhelming worry about how decisions in relationships will impact your future, your partner, and your life. You may feel extreme worry about whether or not you and your partner are on the same page, about what will happen in the future, about compatibility or comparing your relationship to others. These fears and worries can cause emotional distress and distance between you and your partner if not addressed.

Physical Symptoms

Have you ever had a fight with a partner and then got a headache and neck tension afterward? If so, you may have been experiencing some physical symptoms of relationship anxiety. Our mental and physical health are highly intertwined. When we are struggling emotionally it is common for us to also feel physical symptoms. These could include fatigue or exhaustion, restlessness or shaking, feeling nauseous, headaches and tension in your neck and shoulders, and experiencing shortness of breath. Addressing underlying anxiety can help manage physical anxiety symptoms. With that said, if you have any of these symptoms, it is important to consult with your doctor to rule out medical conditions.

What Are the Sources of Anxiety in Relationships?

I have heard many of my clients say, "Why can't I just enjoy this moment?" when they are dating or in relationships. When you are facing relationship anxiety, it can be difficult to be present and instead constantly question yourself, your partner, and your relationship. Where does this anxiety come from? And why do relationships bring out these worries?

Anxiety is often triggered by a stressful life event, and let's be real, relationships can be taxing. When two people with different backgrounds and experiences come together, it is normal to feel anxious about your disparities and what it means for your future. When we reflect on the emotional roots of our relationship anxiety, our worries are often connected to how we have been treated in the past and how we have internalized that treatment. If we have had an abusive or unkind past relationship, or had a difficult dynamic with our parents, we sometimes internalize that information and believe that is what we deserve, making it difficult to move forward in a healthy relationship. Jealousy, insecurity, and past traumas are some of the most common sources of anxiety in relationships. Next, let's dive a little deeper into each of these sources.

Jealousy

Jealousy in relationships occurs when one or both partners perceive a threat and have an overwhelming worry about the other person. Jealousy is a complex emotion and often manifests as anger, irritability, or avoidance in relationships. Jealousy can cause us to be more alert and aware of our partner's behaviors. When we are jealous, we often replay conversations, look through a partner's belongings, or try to find information about their past without talking about it directly. These actions can create distance between you and your partner, create self-esteem issues, and increase your anxiety about the relationship.

Insecurity

All of us have insecurities, but when we combine insecurity with anxiety the feelings can be exacerbated. Insecurity is often described as having a lack of confidence or not feeling good enough. It can create hyperawareness about yourself and how people react to you. It can lead us to believe that our partner or the people we date notice our insecurities the same way we do, and it is difficult for us to believe otherwise. Acknowledging that we are often our own worst critic and our insecurities are something we need to process individually, can be helpful in managing relationship anxiety.

Past Trauma

Unresolved trauma can increase your relationship anxiety drastically. Trauma can shape your beliefs about relationships and can easily trick you into believing all relationships will be the same. If you have had a traumatic romantic relationship or childhood, new relationships can be a major trigger where unresolved feelings are exposed. This may look like jumping to conclusions or forming negative assumptions about your partner. It is important to process your trauma individually with a professional in order to move forward without anxiety in romantic relationships.

ATTACHMENT AND ANXIETY

If you have read up about anxiety in relationships, you may have come across the term "attachment theory" and wondered what it means. It refers to a well-researched and commonly accepted theory in psychology that the degree of security we did or didn't feel as infants and children can deeply affect how we think, feel, and act in relationships later in life.

Psychologist John Bowlby explored parent-child relationships, and his philosophy suggests that there are different attachment styles we develop based on our attachment to our parents as babies and throughout childhood. These will impact us in our romantic relationships as adults. Securely attached people had their needs met when they were young. As adults, they are able to build warm and loving relationships and can communicate needs to their partners. Adults who were not securely attached to their parents can fall into one of the following three attachment styles.

→ *Anxious insecure attached* adults had inconsistent parenting and mixed signals from parents. These individuals received inconsistent emotional connection and developed low self-esteem, so they don't feel worthy of love. They need constant reassurance that they are loved and often deal with relationship anxiety.

→ *Avoidant insecure attached* people had strict and emotionally distant parents who expected their children to be independent. In adulthood, these people are self-sufficient, but in relationships they have difficulty building emotional connection and being emotionally intimate with their partner. They often look for reasons to end a relationship since their parents showed them that people could not be relied on.

→ *Disorganized attachment* occurs when parents are a source of fear or are neglectful. In disorganized attachment the child never knows what to expect from their parents. As adults, they have difficulty letting romantic partners in and expect rejection. Adults with this attachment style have learned that pain in relationships is inevitable.

While the focus of this book is not attachment theory, knowing the basics can provide a useful lens for understanding how your childhood experiences may have influenced your relationships today. You'll find resources on page 137 for learning more about attachment theory. You may even benefit from speaking with a therapist who specializes in the field if it resonates with you.

Behaviors Associated with Relationship Anxiety

If you have been with your partner for some time, you may find yourself feeling nostalgic for "how it used to be." It used to be so steamy, so natural, so fun. Now, more often than not, while on the phone with your partner, you find yourself bingeing the latest Netflix series. Maybe this change causes you to question if you are compatible with your partner, and you find yourself picking fights or avoiding conversations as a result. At every stage, relationships can cause anxiety.

We know we are experiencing relationship anxiety when we begin demonstrating behaviors like seeking reassurance, pushing someone away, avoiding issues, or seeking control. Many of these actions could be qualified as safety behaviors or actions you take in the short term to alleviate anxiety, but ultimately end up causing more distress. Subtle actions to avoid anxiety, like ignoring your partner when they upset you or checking your partner's phone for messages from an ex, may alleviate stress in the moment but are not long-term solutions. Let's discuss some of the more common behaviors associated with relationship anxiety.

Self-Protective Behaviors

Self-protective behaviors are actions you take to protect yourself, your emotions, and your ego. In my practice, I commonly see people who are dating begin to distance themselves from their partner once they start to develop deeper feelings for them. While this behavior might make them feel more protected in the short term, it ultimately denies them the opportunity to build connection in the long term.

You may engage in self-protective behaviors when you feel uncomfortable with the vulnerability in a relationship. It is common to avoid building connections for fear of being hurt or rejected. When we feel this alarm, we push relationships away as a form of protection, creating a self-fulfilling prophecy. When our anxiety urges us to use self-protective factors, we are taking away the opportunity to succeed in a relationship. If we break up with someone in fear that they will never love us, we will never be able to find out if they actually do.

Avoidance Behaviors

Avoidance includes behaviors such as not returning your partner's texts or calls, evading difficult or serious conversations, and convincing yourself that your opinion in the relationship does not matter. Most commonly, avoidance in relationships happens around topics of sex, love, and money.

Avoidant behavior often manifests from fear. Our anxious mind tells us that the best way to protect ourselves from our fears is to avoid conversations around difficult topics or elude our partner altogether. In reality, these actions rob us of the opportunity to have thriving relationships. Working on communication can be a strong place to start conquering avoidance.

Controlling Behaviors

When anxiety strikes, it can make us feel out of control. It is natural for us to start grasping at any control we do have, and sometimes that means trying to dominate our partner. Controlling behaviors can be not allowing your partner to talk to certain people, checking your partner's phone, embarrassing your partner in front of their peers, or dominating conversations without giving your partner space to express themselves. Controlling others may feel good in the moment, but it creates larger relationship issues that can lead to an unhealthy dynamic.

Letting Go of the Past and Looking to the Future

Our past does not define our future, but it can impact our present. In the case study at the beginning of this chapter, Francisco's relationship anxiety was triggered by his fear of having a failed relationship like his parents, even though his current relationship was different. I wonder how the situation would have changed if Francisco had awareness about how his personal history was impacting his anxiety. Take a moment to think about how your past relationships are impacting you now. Do your anxious thoughts get in the way of building connection in relationships?

All relationships are impacted by some form of anxiety, worry, or fear. The ability to reflect on these feelings, understand where they come from, and identify changes you'd like to make is what leads to healing and building healthy connections. Just because you have had anxiety in relationships once does not mean it will always be the case. There are so many tools that you can use to improve your relationships and address your anxiety. You can reflect, use self-help techniques, incorporate coping skills, and seek therapy to work through past anxiety. There is major power in addressing the issue instead of ignoring it.

WHEN IT'S NOT YOU

While this workbook focuses on strategies you can practice for minimizing relationship anxiety in your life, sometimes the worries in your relationship may *not* be about you. In fact, it is common for you to develop some anxieties when your partner has their own issues with the condition. The activity "Whose Anxiety Is It?" on page 55 can help you understand if this may apply to you. If you are comfortable, you may consider inviting your partner to practice some of these exercises with you—or use the communication skills you will learn in this workbook to communicate with them about how their anxiety is impacting you.

If you are in a controlling or abusive relationship, I encourage you to seek resources outside this workbook for help. The exercise "Unhealthy Relationships" on page 44 can help you identify some of the warning signs this might be the case for you. Please refer to the Resources section (page 137) for more information about resources for unhealthy relationships, how to leave unsafe situations, and recovery from relationship abuse. Help is available.

Key Takeaways

We have learned that while anxiety is a normal part of a relationship, it can also cause distress and tension if not addressed. You can identify relationship anxiety by evaluating your behaviors and symptoms and assessing if you are experiencing excessive worries, repetitive thoughts, or fears about your relationship. Your relationship anxiety can manifest physically, emotionally, or mentally and can come from unresolved trauma in past relationships, jealousy, or insecurities.

Relationship anxiety can impact our behaviors and cause us to avoid, control, and self-protect to deter us from feeling pain in relationships. Most important, we learned that there is hope for those of us who have relationship anxiety and that it is possible to work through these issues. Some key takeaways from this chapter include:

- Relationship anxiety is normal and something that can be worked on and improved.

- A core component of addressing relationship anxiety is building communication with our partner.

- A major source of relationship anxiety comes from past romances and unresolved trauma.

- Although vulnerability is difficult, it is necessary for a relationship to develop.

CHAPTER TWO

Self-Discovery and the
Way Forward

IN THIS CHAPTER WE WILL DISCUSS HOW SELF-REFLECTION
and self-discovery are essential in dealing with relationship
anxiety. Self-discovery is a powerful tool but can be challenging
to do. It requires us to step outside ourselves and look at our
actions and behaviors and the reasons behind them. As a step
toward healing, I invite you to reflect on your anxious behaviors
and where they are coming from. We cannot expect others to
understand us if we don't understand ourselves. If you are
identifying anxious behaviors like those discussed in chapter one,
such as avoidance, excessive worries, negative thinking,
and controlling behaviors, it may be time for you to practice
self-reflection.

Anxious behaviors offer some immediate relief but do
not solve the issue. Instead, the goal is to shift to trying to
understand where the worries, fears, and triggers are coming
from. In this chapter we will discuss the importance of this type
of self-exploration and help you consider what factors lead to
anxious moments in your life. We will also discuss some effective
ways to incorporate healthy coping, self-care, and a plan to
combat your relationship anxiety in order to empower yourself
and connect with yourself fully.

The Importance of Self-Work

Now that we have covered some of the behaviors and sources of relationship anxiety, you may be noticing your own issues with it. It is easy to feel overwhelmed thinking about how to work on this part of yourself. The good news is you have a lot of power and control in your healing process. When we take the time to reflect and look deeply at our thought process, we are able to see the *why* behind our actions.

The best way to begin the process of self-reflection is to slow down. We live in a very fast-paced society, and we are constantly thinking of what is coming next. This way of life is not conducive to reflection. In order to connect with your emotions and the reasons behind them it is necessary to slow down, be with yourself, and take time to reflect. Next time you feel your relationship anxiety come up, I encourage you to take time alone to reflect on the root cause. You can ask yourself: *What triggered this reaction? What did this situation remind me of? Where did I learn to respond that way? What vulnerabilities do I have right now that are causing this emotion?*

Understanding yourself and your reactions is the strongest tool you can have in your mental health toolbox. This work is not only important for people in relationships but also for single people and those looking to date. The more awareness we have about ourselves, the easier it is to build healthy relationships.

CASE STUDY | **Theo**

A client I once had—we'll call him Theo—would often discuss how he was frustrated with dating. He was going on three or four dates a week and would rarely go on a second or third date with anyone. He would often blame the dating app algorithm or the people he went out with for not being interesting enough, saying there was no spark.

On one date he noticed that he became so anxious he had to leave the date early. In our next session we discussed common factors in the dates that made him feel that way, and he noticed that people asking him questions about his family was triggering to him. Theo's father had passed away when he was young, and he felt uncomfortable talking about it.

Once he realized this trigger, he was able to process the traumatizing feelings that came with his father's death. He learned how to practice coping skills during dates to tolerate his discomfort, and he was able to see that his relationship anxiety wasn't really about the person he was dating but more about his own experiences. Being able to reflect on how he processes emotions and how his own traumas were impacting him allowed him to open up in relationships and get past the second date.

Developing Healthy Coping Strategies

Coping strategies are another important part of your toolbox for managing relationship anxiety. We all have a lot to juggle in life: family, friends, work, health, etc. No wonder adding relationships to this list can cause so much stress. Getting in touch with how much capacity you have on any given day is a helpful strategy, and using a stoplight metaphor can help us understand what capacity level we have. If your capacity level is green, then you feel emotionally healthy and able to manage stress well. Yellow capacity means you are starting to feel stressed or overwhelmed and need to slow down. If you identify in the red you have no room for additional stress. Using coping skills in the green and yellow level, before you reach your capacity, can be preventive for burnout and anxiety. Each person will have coping skills that work best for them, and some, such as saying mantras, keeping a journal, meditating, or incorporating self-care, can be especially beneficial in managing relationship anxiety.

Keeping a Journal

For some people, keeping a journal is a healthy way to process emotions. A 2018 study demonstrated that people who journaled experienced reduced mental distress, decreased anxiety, less perceived stress, and greater personal resilience compared to those who didn't. When we write down our feelings, it gives us time to release emotion, as well as work through emotional challenges. After arguments we often feel hot and have difficulty regulating emotions. If we have conversations during this period, we can be impulsive in our reactions. Taking the time to journal through our feelings before reacting helps us emotionally regulate and work through our relationship anxiety. In this workbook, you will find some prompts with space to write down your responses on the page. This may form the basis of a journaling practice you can continue beyond these pages.

Mindful Meditation

Meditation can be a helpful tool in minimizing relationship anxiety. Taking time out of the day to reflect on the current moment can help us slow down and see things for what they are. We often are worried about the future and what is ahead instead of the present. Refocusing on the current moment feels so much more manageable and less anxious. You can practice mindful meditation on an app or YouTube, or you can practice on your own by focusing on your breathing. This can be made easier by incorporating mantras. The next time you are practicing meditation, try saying to yourself "I'm breathing in peace" on the inhale and "I'm breathing out stress" on the exhale to help you manage your relationship anxiety.

Embracing Self-Care

Finding what makes you feel good and healthy is an important part of the healing process. Self-care looks different for everyone, and tasks as simple as reading, going for a walk, or taking time to make a budget can be self-care activities. The important part of this practice is finding something that gives you rest and energizes you versus taking energy away from you. In relationships, we get sucked into focusing on ourselves as a couple or unit and sometimes wander away from what makes us as individuals thrive. Incorporating activities that build you up and fill your cup help minimize relationship anxiety.

Asking for Help and Support

So many of us have been taught to not talk about our problems or to not burden people with our issues. This way of thinking isn't helpful. Talking to a friend about your relationship anxiety or opening up to family member can be wildly freeing. By telling someone with whom you feel safe about what you are going through, you are giving yourself an opportunity to be validated. When other people can relate to you or show understanding, it helps lessen anxious thoughts. Once you open up about what you are going through, it is much easier to ask for help, support, or suggestions from the people you love.

FINDING THE RIGHT THERAPIST FOR YOU

Therapy can help you explore patterns in your life that have added to your relationship anxiety and find reassurance and healing. Locating a therapist may take some exploration before finding the right fit for you, which would be someone who makes you feel listened to and safe. You should feel comfortable discussing difficult topics without judgment in therapy. Although this process may take time, know that by reaching out and starting the process you have taken a major step in your mental health journey.

One way to explore this can be through a consultation where you can speak to your potential therapist and describe what you'd like to discuss in therapy and find out if the professional has experience treating your symptoms. During the consultation you can also ask questions about expertise, cultural competency (the ability to understand, respect, and interact with people from all cultures, backgrounds, and belief systems), availability, and cost. Therapy can help you deal with relationship anxiety by helping you process past trauma and relationships that may be holding you back, as well as enable you to build coping skills, develop emotional regulation, and understand where your anxiety comes from. The Resources section on page 137 has more information on how to find the right therapist for you.

Breaking the Cycle of Anxiety and Reshaping Your Relationships

Above all, I want you to know that it is absolutely possible to move forward from relationship anxiety and develop healthy relationships. While there are many ways to work through relationship anxiety, I will be outlining strategies that I have found beneficial for my clients. In order to deal with your relationship anxiety, you must first understand the roots of your anxieties and your triggers. Once you have a deeper understanding of your behavior and where it comes from, it is important to practice compassion for yourself and work toward building your confidence. As your confidence grows, communication and boundary setting will become easier, and hard conversations won't feel as difficult. The final step in reshaping your relationship is to reclaim your joy in being with your partner. We will explore each of these steps further in the upcoming chapters. Each step will have exercises to practice and incorporate into your relationship. Before we get into it, take a moment to thank yourself for taking this step in improving your relationship anxiety. Feel your hope for change begin to resurface.

Identifying the Root of Your Anxieties

With knowledge comes power, and with a deeper understanding of yourself and your anxiety comes more power to change. It might not be fun to sit in your emotions and explore difficult feelings, but doing so can give you a lot of information. When you are emotionally activated and find yourself having an anxious reaction, use coping skills and then reflect. You can ask yourself, "Why am I feeling this way?" "What experience is this situation reminding me of?" or "Where have I heard this anxious voice before?" These questions help us get in touch with the roots of our anxious thoughts.

Understanding Your Triggers

Once you understand some of the root causes of your relationship anxiety, you will also begin to identify certain triggers that enhance it. Triggers can be images, smells, certain words, situations, or vulnerabilities you have that lead to an adverse emotional reaction. A practice that can be helpful for identifying triggers is writing down the anxious behaviors that happened and then working backward and reflecting on what led up to your anxiety. Did you have a good night's rest the night before? Did anything make you uncomfortable? Who did you speak to and what did they say before the emotional outburst? Our history often plays a big role in what triggers us, and understanding that can help us emotionally regulate and minimize anxiety.

Practicing Self-Compassion

Having self-compassion means being able to relate to yourself in a way that's forgiving, accepting, and loving when situations may be less than optimal, just as you would to a good friend. For many of us, being compassionate to ourselves feels awkward and uncomfortable and can bring up feelings of shame. The best advice is to practice. Practice self-compassion on your own, in your head, in front of the mirror. You can start by saying to yourself "I am proud of you" or "Wow, you've been dealing with a lot." This self-compassion is a powerful tool in healing. When you have compassion for yourself you are able to immediately lower your anxiety and have more resilience to cope with stressful events.

Rebuilding Your Self-Confidence

As you incorporate self-compassion, your self-confidence will also improve. It's possible that past relationships have caused you to have a decreased self-esteem if your partner was abusive, manipulative, or unkind. The way you feel about yourself affects your relationship because people feed on your confidence. When we are more confident, we attract people who value us because we believe we deserve to be valued. Building self-confidence helps minimize relationship anxiety as well as our general anxiety.

Knowing Your Boundaries and Communicating Your Needs

A healthy part of any relationship, boundaries are the rules and guidelines we set up that determine how we are treated. Sometimes setting them can be difficult if you have been in unhealthy or codependent relationships where it was difficult to see yourself as an individual. You might set a boundary with a partner when they are raising their voice, discussing hurtful topics, or saying unkind words. Boundaries are often difficult to communicate, and it's easy to avoid setting them. The most important part of boundaries is communication. As uncomfortable as these conversations are, communication is a crucial part of a relationship. Remember that communication builds connection and avoidance creates distance.

Reclaiming Your Joy in Relationships

When we have relationship anxiety, we may notice that we are less joyful or even become depressed because it can feel so overwhelming. Once you have incorporated some of the steps discussed so far, it's important to take time to reclaim your joy and remember what brought it to your relationship. Remember the first time you and your partner met and what made you happy together. It is important to be intentional with reclaiming your joy and talk to your partner about ways you can do this together.

Key Takeaways

In this chapter, we have reviewed the importance of self-discovery and self-awareness in healing from relationship anxiety. Self-discovery can start with the use of coping strategies like journaling, meditation, and self-care to get in touch with the reasons behind our feelings. When we understand where the roots of our anxiety and our triggers come from, we can move forward into healing. Being kind and compassionate to ourselves helps us build confidence to set boundaries and build communication in our relationships. The more we are able to communicate in our relationship, the more we build healthy foundations. Some key takeaways from this chapter include:

- It is important to start using coping strategies when we have capacity and are at a green or yellow light.

- When we have an understanding of our anxiety and triggers, we have more power to change our behavior.

- Setting boundaries is a critical part of forming healthy relationships.

- It is absolutely possible to move forward from relationship anxiety and develop healthy and secure relationships. Read on to take the next step in doing exactly this.

PART TWO

Addressing the Anxiety in Your Relationship

CONGRATULATIONS ON TAKING THIS STEP IN ADDRESSING your anxiety. Once you understand that you have relationship anxiety, you may be asking yourself "What now?" or "What do I do with this information?" Part 2 of this workbook is here to help you take a deeper look at the anxiety in your relationship, where it comes from, and how to heal from it. We will cover how to identify the roots of your anxiety, understand your triggers, practice self-compassion, rebuild self-confidence, know your boundaries and communication needs, and reclaim joy in relationships.

Each chapter will provide exercises, practices, and reflections to assist you in connecting with your feelings in order to learn more about yourself and your relationship anxiety. It's important to remember that you are the expert on your feelings, and being honest and true to yourself in these exercises can be helpful in your healing process. I encourage you to use the exercises to connect with yourself with an open mind and allow the process to assist you in alleviating your relationship anxiety.

CHAPTER THREE

Identifying the Roots of Your Anxieties

BUILDING AN UNDERSTANDING OF WHERE EMOTIONS COME FROM IS an integral part of the healing process. The more we understand the roots of our feelings, the more power we have to adjust and change those feelings. When we understand our anxieties, we feel empowered to heal from them. The practices, exercises, and reflections in this chapter are designed to assist you in connecting with your emotions to identify some of the root causes of your feelings.

In addition to identifying feelings, the prompts and reflections are designed to help you look objectively at past and present relationships that may have impacted your feelings today. It can be emotional to connect with yourself in this way, so this chapter has incorporated several self-soothing and self-regulating strategies to assist you as you reflect. My hope is that this chapter will open your eyes to themes in your life that have led to your relationship anxiety so that you have a deeper understanding of where it is coming from.

CASE STUDY | **Cameo and Dev**

Cameo and Dev have been dating for three years and are in an overall secure and healthy relationship. Cameo's fortieth birthday is coming up, and she wants to plan something special. She is secretly hoping that Dev plans something for her. As the date gets closer, Cameo mentions, "My birthday is coming up in a few weeks, what do you think we should do?" When Dev responds saying, "Oh, I hadn't even thought about it," Cameo notices a strong physical response: She feels her stomach get upset and nauseous. She feels like isolating and runs to the bathroom to be alone.

Cameo's mother was in and out of her life and would often forget it was her birthday. Cameo would always do the planning for her three younger siblings' birthdays, and hers was rarely celebrated. When she met Dev, she loved that they would do things together for her birthday and felt taken aback that Dev hadn't planned anything. Cameo hasn't shared with Dev that she had to do a lot of processing and self-work to get to the point where she feels worthy of even celebrating her birthday. For Cameo, this moment was especially difficult because it felt similar to traumatic times in her childhood when she felt isolated and alone.

Dev was surprised by Cameo's reaction and went to the bathroom to check on her. Because Cameo has explored the roots of her anxiety through self-work, she was able to talk to her partner about her feelings. After talking, Dev clarified that no birthday plans had been made because of some anxiety Dev has been feeling personally. Dev was able to validate Cameo's feelings and share excitement about her upcoming birthday. This made Cameo feel safe again, and they were able to plan her birthday celebration together.

RELATIONSHIP ANXIETY QUIZ

Take this quiz to find out if you might have relationship anxiety. Score yourself using this rating scale:

0 = never, 1 = rarely, 2 = sometimes, 3 = frequently, 4 = often, 5 = always

1. Do you fear that you will never be in a healthy relationship? _____

2. Do you worry about your partner leaving you? _____

3. Do you avoid getting into relationships in fear that it won't work out? _____

4. Do you feel consumed with negative thoughts about your relationship or dating? _____

5. Do you avoid having difficult conversations with your partner? _____

6. Do you notice an increase in concentration issues, problems sleeping, distraction, and irritability? _____

7. Do you worry about your compatibility with your partner and if they are good enough for you? _____

8. Do you feel jealous or insecure in your relationship? _____

9. Do you feel triggered in your current relationship or when dating because of unhealthy past relationships? _____

10. Do you find yourself trying to control your partner? _____

TOTAL SCORE: _____

Understanding your score:

- 20 or below: It seems like you are able to manage anxious thoughts. It is always helpful to learn tools, and this book can help keep you on track.

- 21–30: It seems you may have mild relationship anxiety and maybe some worrisome thoughts about relationships. Use this workbook to build your insight on where some of these thoughts are coming from.

- 31–40: Relationship anxiety seems to be impacting you most of the time. This workbook is a great place to start learning tools to manage those feelings.

- 40 or over: Relationship anxiety is impacting your daily thoughts and feelings. This book and connecting with a therapist is a good starting place.

TAKE A MINDFUL WALK

Practicing mindfulness can be helpful in centering yourself and better managing your thoughts. Mindfulness allows us to be in the present moment without judgment or attachment, as well as helps reduce pain, tension, and stress. The practice of taking a mindful walk can assist you in building your focus and better prepare you to explore the roots of your relationship anxiety. This practice can be done anywhere and only takes a few minutes. When you have a moment, take time to follow the directions and complete your mindful walk.

1. Choose a safe place to take a walk.

2. As you begin your walk, take several deep breaths, breathing in through your nose and out through your mouth.

3. Notice your stomach rise as you breathe in and lower as you breathe out.

4. As you breathe in, say the words "I am present" to yourself.

5. As you breathe out, imagine yourself blowing away distractions.

6. Notice the things around you. What do you hear? What do you see? What do you smell?

7. What are you noticing that you haven't noticed before?

8. If distracting thoughts present themselves, acknowledge them and then refocus on your walk.

9. Continue to focus on your senses and what you are noticing throughout your walk.

10. As your walk comes to an end, bring yourself back to your breath.

11. When your walk has concluded, take a moment to think about how you feel. Do you feel more centered than before the walk? Make note if this was a helpful exercise for you.

 My past relationships do not define my current or future relationships.

Sometimes anxiety is so much a part of our daily lives we don't even realize we have relationship anxiety until it is pointed out to us. It can be difficult to identify the roots of our anxiety when it has become such a normal feeling. Take some time to reflect. Can you think of the first time you noticed your relationship anxiety? What were you doing? What was the anxiety about? How did your body feel in those anxious moments? Describe your experience here.

FEELINGS CHECKLIST

Relationships bring up many feelings. From love to hate and everything in between, it is common to feel a wide array of emotions in a relationship, as well as experience two opposite feelings in the same relationship. Getting in touch with your feelings and being able to label them helps build a deeper understanding of yourself. What have you felt in previous or current relationships?

☐ Anger   ☐ Joy

☐ Annoyance   ☐ Love

☐ Anxiety   ☐ Panic

☐ Attraction   ☐ Pleasure

☐ Disconnection   ☐ Rejection

☐ Envy   ☐ Resentment

☐ Excitement   ☐ Self-consciousness

☐ Frustration   ☐ Self-protectiveness

☐ Guilt   ☐ Shame

☐ Hurt   ☐ Suspicion

☐ Infatuation   ☐ Uneasiness

☐ Jealousy

FINDING CALM WITH
DIAPHRAGMATIC BREATHING

The diaphragm is the muscle under your lungs that contracts when you breathe and optimizes your oxygen intake. Diaphragmatic breathing is an effective way to build relaxation, slow your heartbeat, and stabilize your blood pressure. It has also been shown to lower levels of stress hormones in the body and minimize anxiety. Take a moment alone to practicing diaphragmatic breathing to regulate your emotions and connect with yourself.

This practice can help you get comfortable with exploring your relationship anxiety on a deeper level in this moment. It is also a skill you can use in your relationship when you become anxious. Follow these step-by-step instructions to begin.

1. Sit in a comfortable position.

2. Relax your shoulders away from your ears.

3. Place one hand on your chest and the other on your stomach.

4. Begin taking deep breaths in through your nose and feel your stomach rise while your chest remains still.

5. Exhale through your mouth slowly, blowing the air out, and feel your stomach begin to lower back down.

6. Repeat ten to fifteen times or for five to ten minutes.

 I am connected to myself and my feelings. I am aware of my emotions and their roots.

WHAT ATTACHMENT STYLE DO I HAVE?

In chapter one, we briefly explored the concept of attachment styles (page 9). These are the forms of attachment that we develop with our caregivers in childhood that influence our relationships as adults.

Place a check next to the statements you identify with. The column where you have the most check marks will show you what attachment style you may have.

SECURE

☐ I find it easy to be affectionate with my partner.

☐ I feel comfortable depending on my romantic partners.

☐ I am generally satisfied with my romantic relationships.

☐ When I get in an argument with my partner, we are able to recover quickly.

☐ When I disagree with someone, I feel comfortable sharing my opinion.

☐ I am generally satisfied in my relationship.

Total: _____

ANXIOUS INSECURE

☐ I worry that if my partner leaves me, I won't find someone else.

☐ If I notice my partner acting differently, I automatically think I did something wrong.

☐ I often worry that one day my partner won't love me anymore.

☐ When my partner is away, I fear they will meet someone else and leave me.

☐ When I express my feelings to my partner, I worry they won't feel the same.

☐ I worry I'm not attractive enough.

Total: _____

AVOIDANT INSECURE

☐ I'm fine the next day after a breakup.

☐ It's hard for me to emotionally support my partner.

☐ My independence is most important to me.

☐ I prefer not to share my deepest feelings.

☐ My partner wants intimacy more than I do.

☐ I don't like when people depend on me.

Total: _____

Now that you have identified your possible attachment style, you have developed insight into the *why* behind some of your anxious behaviors within relationships. Learning more about your particular attachment style can help you identify partners who can meet your needs, as well as enable you to better communicate your needs to others. Insight about attachment styles in general can also assist you in developing more secure relationships in adulthood.

ASSUMPTIONS AND CORE BELIEFS

Assumptions and core beliefs can deeply impact our relationships. Core beliefs are absolute statements about ourselves, others, or the world that impact our life and how we think about everything around us. Core beliefs learned in our past can be helpful for understanding our relationship anxiety. While these attitudes can be positive and uplifting, when they are negative and self-critical, they hold us back. Check any of the core beliefs that you feel aligned with or write down your own at the end of the list.

☐ I am weak.

☐ I am unlovable.

☐ I will end up alone.

☐ No one likes me.

☐ People can't be trusted.

☐ I am a failure.

☐ Nothing ever goes right.

☐ The world is dangerous.

☐ I'm not good enough.

☐ Other: _____

☐ Other: _____

☐ Other: _____

Now that you have identified your possible core beliefs, know that it is 100 percent possible to relearn them and identify a more helpful way to self-identify. One of the ways to begin this process is by examining the evidence. For example, if your core belief is that no one likes you, are there times in your life where people have shown interest in you? When people have hung out with you? Invited you somewhere? That evidence helps in disproving the core belief.

Choose the negative core belief you most align with and list all the evidence you can think of that proves it is not 100 percent true:

_____

_____

_____

_____

LEARNING TO SELF-SOOTHE

Practicing self-soothing is a helpful skill to better regulate your feelings. Thinking about the roots of our anxiety and attachment styles can create irritability, tension, and other intense emotions. As you work through this workbook, be sure to take time to self-soothe and practice coping skills. Everyone has different strategies that work for them, so I encourage you to try as many techniques as possible to find what works for you. Following is a list of possible self-soothing practices. All of these can be done in three minutes or less and fit into a variety of schedules. Once you have tried them all, highlight the ones that worked best for you.

- Splash cold water on your face

- Draw for three minutes

- Go on a short walk

- Call someone who makes you happy

- Make a list of three to five things you are grateful for

- Pet your animal

- Watch a funny video

- Put your feet in the grass

- Dance to one song

- Write down one positive affirmation for yourself

- Rip up paper

- Organize one drawer in your home

- Stretch

- Light your favorite candle

- Hug yourself

YOUR PAST RELATIONSHIPS

It is totally normal for past relationships to impact our current ones. Even if we have moved on, we often take pieces of old relationships with us because they have been ingrained in our thoughts and experiences. It can be powerful to reflect on past experiences that have impacted our anxiety about relationships. Write about a time you felt anxious in a past romantic union, friendship, or family relationship. Do you think about this relationship often? What parts of that relationship are you carrying with yourself now?

What did you learn from that situation? In what ways is this information helpful for you to manage your relationship anxiety now?

HOW TO SHIFT ANXIOUS THOUGHTS

We all have thoughts that impact us daily, and negative ones can especially influence our relationship anxiety and how we build connection. Take a moment to think about some of the anxious thoughts that pop up in your head regularly. Write four of these thoughts in the anxious thought column in the table provided. Now begin to think about alternative thoughts that can replace the negative ones. Try not to think about each alternative thought as a positive and cheerful one. Instead, think of it as a realistic—or more neutral—thought. Write the alternative thoughts in the right-hand column and notice if your anxiety decreased.

ANXIOUS THOUGHT	ALTERNATIVE THOUGHT
Example: They never leave their phone alone, so they must be texting someone else.	Maybe they like having their phone close to them the same way most of my friends do. Maybe it doesn't mean anything.

VISUALIZING A JOYFUL RELATIONSHIP

Visualization is a powerful tool in healing from relationship anxiety. It can happen by closing your eyes and thinking through what healing looks like in detail. Take a moment to picture yourself in a happy and healthy relationship. What does that look like for you? How do you feel in that relationship? What are you doing with your partner that brings you joy?

The following practice uses specific imagery to help you better visualize overcoming your relationship anxiety.

1. Try visualizing yourself as a tree with roots at this moment. The roots below you show you where your relationship anxiety is coming from.

2. Visualize yourself reaching down to those roots and seeing them up close. See what the roots are connected to.

3. Envision yourself understanding the roots of your anxiety and being able to come to peace with them.

4. Picture that helping you develop healthy relationships.

5. Imagine yourself full of understanding and more connected to yourself than ever before. Feel the sense of empowerment that will bring to you.

6. Finally, tell yourself that this level of insight and understanding is possible for you, and you are closer to it than ever before.

LOOKING AT THE ROOTS

Let's talk about the roots to your current relationship anxiety. Write down some of the tree roots you were able to visualize from the last exercise. Where did the anxiety you are currently experiencing originate from? Is it a past relationship, something you heard as a child that you internalized, or worries about your future? Take a moment to think about the root of the issue. What past experiences have you internalized? What stories are you telling yourself that increase your anxiety? When you experience anxiety in your current relationships, where do you think that anxiety is coming from?

....

....

....

....

....

....

....

....

....

....

....

....

....

....

THOUGHTS, FEELINGS, AND BEHAVIORS

Our thoughts, feelings, and behaviors are interconnected. The cognitive triangle is a tool we use to see that connection. The following image of this triangle demonstrates how our thoughts, feelings, and behaviors depend on each other. For example, your thought might be "I know I'm not a good partner, and it's just a matter of time until they leave me." The feeling is increased anxiety, and the behavior is that you withdraw from your partner so that you don't upset them.

But if your thought changes to, "Actually, sometimes I am a good partner," then the feeling might be pride and the behavior is to plan a date out with your partner. The cognitive triangle truly shows the power of our thoughts.

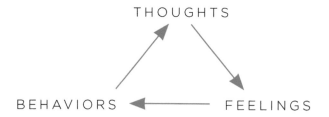

Write down an anxious thought you commonly have that impacts your relationship, as well as a corresponding feeling and behavior:

Thought:

....

....

....

Feeling:

....

....

....

Behavior:

....

....

....

Now write down an alternative, more neutral thought and how it would impact the feeling and behavior:

Thought:

....

....

....

Feeling:

....

....

....

Behavior:

....

....

....

What change occurred when you shifted your thought?

....

....

....

UNHEALTHY RELATIONSHIPS

Have you ever felt like you are the only one working on your relationship and no matter how much you do, the same problems continue to happen? This may be a sign for you to reflect on whether you are in an unhealthy relationship. If you have a partner who is unkind, controlling, manipulative, or abusive, I encourage you to seek support outside this book. The Resources section of this book will have additional supportive resources (see page 137).

The following exercise is designed to help you identify if you are in a healthy or unhealthy relationship. Check off statements that are happening in your relationship.

☐ Your partner makes all the decisions and often tells you what to do.

☐ Your partner is unreasonable and jealous.

☐ Your partner tries to isolate you from family or friends.

☐ You don't feel comfortable sharing your feelings with your partner.

☐ You feel that your partner is constantly picking fights with you.

☐ Your partner talks down to you using unkind language.

☐ Your partner lies to you.

☐ Your partner makes fun of your interests and opinions.

☐ Your partner destroys your belongings.

☐ Your partner threatens to do something drastic if the relationship ends.

☐ Your partner uses physical force to get their way.

☐ You feel pressure or feel forced to engage in sexual behavior with your partner.

If any of these items were checked off for you, I encourage you to visit the Resources section in the back of this workbook (page 137). When you experience an unhealthy relationship, it is important to get support and process with someone safe what next steps you should take. There is a spectrum of unhealthy relationships, meaning there are some characteristics that can be worked on through communication and therapy and some that are unsafe to work through. Connecting with a therapist will help you better understand your current situation. If you feel you are in immediate danger or need additional support, please call the National Domestic Violence hotline at 800-799-7233.

QUICK QUESTIONS

We have completed several exercises to assist you in reflecting on the roots of your anxiety. Try to complete this one by filling in the blank with the first thing that comes to mind.

When I am anxious in my relationship, I:

I learned anxious behavior from:

My parents' or caregivers' relationship taught me:

I have learned that healthy relationships occur by:

My past relationships have taught me:

In my relationships, I tend to feel:

My relationship anxiety largely comes from:

Key Takeaways

Understanding the root of your relationship anxiety is an empowering experience that can help you through the healing process. All of us have experiences that we carry from past relationships and traumas. The goal is not to avoid this process but to be in touch with what we are carrying with us and realize how it impacts us. This chapter has helped you get in touch with the emotions that occur in relationships and has demonstrated how anxiety and attachment styles impact our relationships. We have also explored how our thoughts affect our relationships and how to build alternative thoughts to manage some of the relationship anxiety. Some key takeaways from this chapter include:

- It is normal for past relationships to impact our current ones.

- Self-soothing and coping strategies are important to incorporate into the healing process.

- You can feel two opposite emotions in one relationship.

- Visualization is a powerful tool for connecting with ourselves.

- Neutralizing your negative thoughts can have a positive impact on your relationship anxiety.

- It is possible to overcome limiting self-beliefs and find more joy in relationships.

CHAPTER FOUR

Understanding Your Triggers

IN THE WORLD OF MENTAL HEALTH, A TRIGGER IS SOMETHING THAT evokes an emotional reaction and affects your emotional state. Triggers often involve an intense or uncomfortable emotional reaction that is rooted in a past experience. Being able to understand our triggers can help us manage our relationship anxiety.

Many emotional triggers in relationships stem from negative experiences in the past that led to feelings of jealousy, insecurity, and avoidance. In this chapter you will learn how to identify your triggers, explore why you feel negative emotions, and reflect on patterns of behavior. We will also cover skills that can help you avoid being triggered in your current relationship situation.

This chapter includes prompts, exercises, affirmations, and practices formulated to help you work through your triggers and continue to heal. By the end of this chapter, you should have a strong sense of your triggers, coping skills to manage them, and an understanding of how to shift your thoughts to better manage your relationship anxiety.

CASE STUDY | **Morgan**

Morgan has been married to her wife for a little over a year. She often talks about how happy she is in her relationship and how she doesn't deserve her wife. Morgan was married previously for three years and was divorced after her partner cheated on her. In her past relationship, Morgan's partner would demean her and talk down to her, often calling her unkind names.

Morgan has been working with a therapist for several years and feels good in her current relationship. Anytime Morgan notices a change in her wife's behavior, she automatically becomes anxious and worried, which often leads to her secretly searching through her wife's phone. When this happens, Morgan often begins to worry that her wife is cheating on her and feels like she will never be good enough for anyone.

Even though Morgan has worked through her past with a therapist, there are still times when she feels triggered by it. These triggers often lead to her creating distance in her relationship even though nothing negative is happening in her current marriage. When Morgan talks to her therapist about this, they begin to examine themes in the situations and work toward processing some of her fears about infidelity and failure. By doing this, Morgan can identify moments when she may be triggered and use coping strategies to manage her fears. This change has helped her anxiety and led to a healthier relationship.

WHAT TRIGGERS YOU?

People can be triggered by many different things depending on their history and experiences. Knowing your triggers can help you prevent instability and emotional outbursts. While it is common to try to avoid things that upset you, it is much more beneficial to address the triggers and try to understand them. The first step in this process is being able to identify them, although this can be difficult at first.

   Here is a list of common triggers for people. Take a moment to read each one aloud and reflect on if this is something that normally impacts you. Be aware of your body's reactions when reading these aloud. Check the triggers you identify with most.

☐ Feeling rejected or betrayed

☐ Feeling out of control emotionally

☐ Being excluded or ignored

☐ Being criticized

☐ Feeling unwanted or unneeded

☐ Loss of independence

☐ A lack of affection

☐ Feeling lonely

☐ Feeling manipulated

☐ Lack of trust

☐ Feeling unsafe

☐ Feeling like you can't speak up for yourself

 I am connected to my feelings and
where they come from.

LOOKING AT YOUR EXPERIENCES

Let's start to think about what often triggers your relationship anxiety. Take a moment to reflect on what type of stress triggers anxiety within your relationship or when dating. What are common situations in which you become anxious? Does your partner impact your anxiety? Does your partner also have their own anxiety? Focus on themes that come up for you during bouts of anxiety. Describe some of the triggers that come up for you in relationships.

_____

_____

_____

_____

_____

_____

_____

_____

_____

_____

_____

_____

_____

_____

YOU CAN VALIDATE YOURSELF

Validation is acknowledging that another person's emotions, thoughts, and behaviors are understandable. It can improve relationships and interpersonal effectiveness. You may validate a peer by saying "I can see why you feel that way" or "That sounds frustrating."

Sometimes we need validation in anxious moments but may not have people around us who are able to provide us with it at that time. Self-validation can be especially helpful in these situations, allowing us to regulate our emotions and feel more confident.

Practice self-validation by describing your own experience, point of view, or emotions and validating the pieces that are true by encouraging yourself, treating yourself with kindness, and noticing and accepting your feelings. Some examples of self-validation are saying "I don't feel heard right now, and that's why I'm feeling anxious" or "I can understand why I feel anxious in this relationship at times."

Take a few moments to validate yourself and your experiences now. Reflect on how self-validation is helpful to you.

TRIGGER TABLE

Now that you have some awareness about what is triggering to you, let's talk about how we can manage those things that cause anxiety. Being able to write down your triggers can be a helpful way to work through them. Once you become aware and are able to identify them, I encourage you to use coping skills (like those in "Learning to Self-Soothe" on page 37). This can help with slowing down your body and your reactions.

In the boxes provided, write down the date, the trigger you identified, if you were able to use a coping skill and what it was, and the result of the situation. When the table is full, reflect on the outcomes of situations. Ask yourself if the coping skills were helpful in slowing down your reactions and what coping skills were most helpful for you.

DATE	TRIGGER	DID YOU USE A COPING SKILL? WHAT WAS IT?	RESULT
Example: Monday	Not feeling appreciated after cooking dinner for my partner.	Yes. Deep breaths.	I still became upset and got teary, but I expressed my feelings instead of isolating like I usually would.

WHOSE ANXIETY IS IT?

Sometimes we aren't the only one in our relationship with anxiety. Our partners can also contribute to our collective relationship anxiety. When both partners have anxiety, it can be more challenging to understand your triggers. Don't worry—this exercise will help!

In the following images you will see three different situations: one where your partner is highly anxious; one where your partner has a medium level of anxiety; and one where you partner is not anxious at all. Take a moment to visualize a situation (real or imagined) that matches each description and rate what you think your anxiety level would be in response using this scale:

**5 = high anxiety with panic, 4 = high anxiety but no panic,
3 = medium anxiety, 2 = low anxiety, 1 = neutral anxiety, 0 = no anxiety**

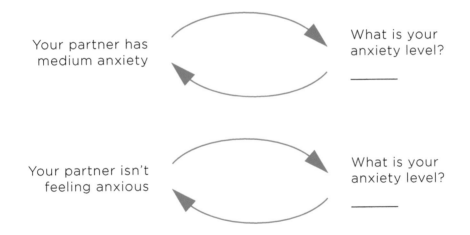

Your partner has medium anxiety

What is your anxiety level?

_____

Your partner isn't feeling anxious

What is your anxiety level?

_____

What do your ratings tell you? Are you someone who is greatly impacted by your partner's anxiety or someone who remains constant no matter what type of anxiety your partner has? This information can be helpful in identifying triggers and managing anxious thoughts. If you are currently in a relationship with somebody whose anxiety is contributing to your own, it could be helpful to discuss it with them so that you can both find the support and resources you need.

REFLECTING ON A SITUATION

Being able to reflect and work through our triggers can be helpful. Reflection allows us to build a deeper understanding of ourselves. Even after the feeling has passed it is helpful to reflect to gain understanding of your emotions. Describe a situation that occurred in the last month that triggered your relationship anxiety. Think about what happened before you were triggered. What was going on in the situation? Who were you with? How did your body react? Once you have reflected on the situation, take time to write about what you think increased your anxiety.

BODY SCAN BREATHING TO EASE STRESS

Often our triggers and stressors manifest physically in our bodies. Take the next three to five minutes to practice body scan breathing to get in touch with your body and release anxiety.

1. Sit in a relaxed position with your feet flat on the floor and palms in your lap.

2. Close your eyes if comfortable.

3. Take several deep breaths, in through your nose and out through your mouth.

4. As you breathe in, begin to notice tension in your body beginning with your head, neck, and shoulders.

5. As you breathe out, try to release the tension by lowering your shoulders, rolling your neck, and softening your facial expression.

6. Continue this all the way down your body, focusing on your chest, torso, legs, and feet. As you breathe in, continue to notice tension, and release the tension and relax your body as you breathe out.

7. Once you have scanned your entire body for tension, begin breathing in and repeat, "I acknowledge my triggers"; then, as you breathe out, repeat, "I release my stress."

8. Repeat these phrases five to ten times.

9. Open your eyes and enjoy the release you feel.

GIVE P.E.A.C.E. A CHANCE

There are so many things that impact our triggers and our reaction to them. One way to work toward regulating emotions is to check in with our bodies. In fact, there is no better way to take care of your mind than through the body. The P.E.A.C.E. acronym helps us remember how we can check in on our physical well-being to help our emotions remain in check. If one of these areas is not getting attention it can contribute to emotional outbursts or feeling more triggered than usual. I encourage you to take time to regularly check in on how you are attending to P.E.A.C.E. If you notice there are areas that have been causing difficulty, put additional attention there.

- **P**hysical illness—Check in with yourself to see how your body is doing physically and make sure to see your doctors regularly and take any prescribed medication to keep your body healthy.

- **E**ating balanced—Remember that food nourishes our entire body and is necessary to be able to function effectively. Eating regularly, staying hydrated, and being aware of foods that make you more emotional are important parts of caring for ourselves.

- **A**void drugs and alcohol—Moderation is always important, and awareness of how our body reacts to certain substances is crucial for our health. For many people alcohol and drugs increase anxious thoughts and worries.

- **C**onsistent sleep—Not getting enough sleep often exacerbates our symptoms and makes us feel tired, irritable, and lethargic. Trying to get the standard eight hours of sleep at night and keeping a consistent sleep schedule helps our mental health.

- **E**xercise—Moving your body daily can help you release pent-up anxiety and feel more capable to take on daily stressors.

DISTRACTION CARD

There are times when distraction can be a healthy coping skill. It can be challenging to discuss our triggers and think about past traumatic events. Using coping skills is always helpful, but there will be times when you may find it more helpful to distract yourself instead.

It is okay to use distraction in moderation when feeling overwhelmed or unable to process our thoughts in the moment. With that said, it is important that we do not use distraction as our only coping skill and that we continue to work on our anxiety directly.

Some of my favorite forms of distraction are to organize myself or part of my room, practice grounding by putting my feet on grass and being mindful of the sensations around me, or doing a craft like painting or drawing. These strategies help me self-soothe, refocus, and regulate.

Write down six distraction strategies that you can use to minimize anxiety and triggers.

When I feel triggered and feel my anxiety increase, I can distract myself by:

- ....
  ....

- ....
  ....

- ....
  ....

- ....
  ....

- ....
  ....

- ....
  ....

CHAIN ANALYSIS

A chain analysis can help us understand our behavior and our triggers. It involves the following steps.

1. **Anxious behavior:** Identify the anxious behavior. Describe what occurred in a detailed way. *Example: I said, "I don't think this is working" and walked away after thinking my partner was not interested in me anymore.*

2. **Prompting event:** Describe the prompting event that led to the anxious behavior. *Example: My partner didn't return my text and I was waiting five hours for them to respond after I asked them if they wanted to come meet my parents.*

3. **Vulnerabilities:** Describe any factors that may have caused you to be vulnerable to anxiety (P.E.A.C.E.). *Example: I only slept five hours the night before because I had an important work deadline.*

4. **Links:** Describe the chain of events or links that happened to lead up to the anxious behavior. This can be actions you took, bodily sensations, feelings, and emotions. *Examples:*

   - *I assumed he didn't want to meet my parents and was avoiding me.*

   - *I felt nauseous and angry.*

   - *I started to think that I am better than this treatment.*

5. **Consequences:** What are the consequences of the anxious behavior? How did you or your partner react? How did you feel after? What was the outcome? *Examples:*

   - *My partner was angry and didn't understand why I was trying to end our relationship.*

   - *We had an argument.*

   - *I felt sad and lonely.*

Now, think of a difficult situation from a relationship that you would like to analyze to better understand your behaviors and triggers. Then fill out the following chain analysis table to better understand where your anxiety was coming from.

	DESCRIPTION
ANXIOUS BEHAVIOR	
PROMPTING EVENT	
VULNERABILITIES	
LINKS	
CONSEQUENCES	

CHANGING YOUR RESPONSE

Think about a triggering situation for you. What occurred in this situation? Describe it here, including your anxious behaviors. Was there an alternative behavior you could have used? Could you have slowed down your reaction to minimize your anxiety?

....

....

....

....

Now take time to rewrite how the situation and consequences would have been different if your behavior was different. What is the consequence now? How are your feelings impacted when your behavior changes?

....

....

....

....

....

 I am at peace. I feel calm and able to manage my emotions.

WHAT DO YOU NEED?

Use this exercise to get in touch with your needs and build your understanding of yourself. Remember that you are an expert on *you* and know best what you need in any given moment. Don't think hard about your answers—just write down what comes to mind first.

When I feel triggered, I need:

_____

_____

When I'm triggered, I feel:

_____

_____

I feel supported when:

_____

_____

My most useful coping strategy is:

_____

_____

When I'm upset, I wish someone would tell me:

_____

_____

CALMING MEDITATION

When anxious thoughts arise in a relationship, they can get in the way of connecting with your partner and finding joy in everyday experiences. The following meditation will help you redirect yourself from anxious thoughts so that you can live more fully in the present moment. As you focus on your breathing, you will inevitably find that thoughts arise, and that's okay—what's important is how you learn to respond to them.

As you begin this meditation practice, take a moment to thank yourself for being here and participating in this activity. Acknowledge some of the relationship anxiety you feel in this current moment and bring it to your attention. Try to validate your anxiety by telling yourself your feelings are valid and understandable. Take a few moments to center yourself and feel connected to the present moment, then follow these steps.

1. Sit with your palms facing up in your lap and your feet flat on the floor. Take a few deep breaths in and out.

2. Acknowledge any feelings you are experiencing.

3. Continue to take deep breaths in through the nose and out through the mouth.

4. As you continue to breathe, it is possible that anxious thoughts will come up for you. As they come, imagine them on a conveyor belt floating away from you and try to refocus on your breath.

5. Imagine yourself putting your anxiety on the conveyor belt and watching it float away. You can see the anxiety floating in the distance far from you. The farther away it gets, the easier it becomes to breathe.

6. Refocus on your breath and notice the fluidity and ease of your breath. Breathe in peace and breathe out anxiety until you come back to awareness.

Take a moment to congratulate yourself on addressing your anxieties and actively working to heal from them.

Key Takeaways

In this chapter you have taken a deep look into what triggers your relationship anxiety. At this point you understand how triggers impact you and what role your partner's anxiety has in your healing process. An important part of this chapter was being able to work through several stressful situations and think of what you could do differently in the future to avoid the same outcome. In this chapter we continued to practice coping skills to be able to regulate our emotions after discussing triggers, and I encourage you to continue to use coping skills often. Here are some key takeaways from this chapter:

- Using coping skills can help us manage our triggers effectively.

- It is possible that our partner's anxiety is impacting our triggers and relationship anxiety.

- Checking in with our body and physical health and understanding our vulnerabilities are good ways to minimize triggers.

- When we understand our triggers it is easier to change our anxious behavior and incorporate more stability into our relationships.

CHAPTER FIVE

Practicing Self-Compassion

HOW MANY NEGATIVE THOUGHTS DO YOU HAVE ABOUT YOURSELF throughout the day on average? Unfortunately, it is common for people to be their own worst critic, especially in relationships or in dating. Yet practicing self-compassion can be a powerful tool for minimizing relationship anxiety.

In this chapter we will reflect on the benefits of self-compassion and self-love, as well as review exercises that can build your self-care practice. This chapter is designed to be a reminder that it's okay to have empathy and be kind to yourself, that it's healthy to be gentle and talk to yourself the way you would talk to a close friend, and that you should provide space to allow reflection on the things you like about yourself. This will all help you build empathy and compassion in your relationships.

CASE STUDY | **Lorena**

Lorena had her first baby four months ago, and she is generally anxious about taking her newborn out of the house. She has also noticed intensifying worries about her relationship. She started worrying that she didn't marry the right person and often has thoughts about leaving the relationship. These thoughts are frequently followed by negative self-talk that sounds like "How could I think that way? I know I would never find someone else" or "I hate myself for thinking this way. I'm a bad mom."

When Lorena's mom comes over to check on her, Lorena mentions, "I feel like I don't know myself right now. I feel lonely, and I don't know if I can stay in this relationship anymore." Lorena's mom suggests that Lorena needs to take some time for herself outside the house without the baby and offers to babysit for a few hours.

Lorena is able to take a shower without interruption, meet a friend at her favorite lunch spot, and take a few hours to work on some art projects she enjoys. At lunch she shares with her friend how she has been feeling. Her friend validates her feelings by saying, "Of course you feel this way. You have a lot on your plate. Maybe you need to prioritize some time for yourself every week."

Lorena begins to incorporate self-care weekly and practices validating herself and her feelings. After a few weeks she talks to her husband about some of her concerns and makes a plan with him to reconnect.

NEUTRALIZING YOUR NEGATIVE THOUGHTS

You are not alone in feeling anxious about your relationship. It is common for anxious thoughts about our relationships to overcome us. When you are feeling overwhelmed with relationship anxiety, it is easy to be hard on yourself and ask things like "Why am I like this?" or "Why do I have to think this way?" This type of self-talk is common, but it is unhelpful in your healing journey. Instead, it is better to reframe these thoughts to be more compassionate with yourself.

Take a moment to write down some common harmful thoughts you have about your relationship anxiety in the first column. In the second column, write down a reframed alternative thought that is more compassionate toward yourself.

Note: Your neutral reframed thought does not have to be completely positive. Instead, think of it as a slight shift to something more neutral in between positive and negative. See the example provided in the table for ideas.

HARMFUL NEGATIVE THOUGHT	NEUTRAL REFRAMED THOUGHT
Example: "Why can't I just be normal and not worry so much about my relationship?"	"I am struggling with my thoughts right now because I feel really stressed. It's okay to feel this way."

LEANING INTO COMPASSION

Why is it that we are so good at being compassionate to others, but have such difficulty treating ourselves with the same kindness? Self-compassion is demonstrated in how we relate to ourselves during difficult moments and is rooted in messages we received as children about what we are worthy of and how we should care about ourselves. Being compassionate toward ourselves can be uncomfortable at first, but it is a strong protective factor for minimizing anxiety.

Write about a time when someone was compassionate toward you. What did they say? How did that compassion impact you?

_____

_____

_____

_____

Now imagine what it would be like to extend that same compassion to yourself. Would you find it challenging? What benefit would you gain from being kinder to yourself?

_____

_____

_____

_____

LOVING-KINDNESS MEDITATION

"Loving-kindness" is a mindfulness activity that can be particularly helpful in building compassion for yourself. This activity can be focused on anyone, but let's practice spreading loving-kindness to yourself.

When you're in a cycle of negativity, it is easy to use harmful words to describe yourself. Use this loving-kindness meditation to build self-love and self-compassion.

1. Start by sitting, standing, or lying down and take slow, deep breaths in and out for one or two minutes with your palms open and facing up, if comfortable.

2. Focus on yourself by saying your name aloud or in your head and touching your arms and or legs with tenderness.

3. Imagine yourself sending loving positive energy to yourself and wishing yourself the best.

4. Radiate loving-kindness to yourself by reciting the following warm wishes. Take a deep, gentle breath between saying each one.

   - I am sending myself loving-kindness.

   - May I feel safe.

   - May I be healthy.

   - May I feel at peace.

   - May I feel happiness.

   - I am worthy of love and compassion.

   - I will accept love and compassion from others.

Think of any other phrases of loving-kindness you can say and recite them to yourself before completing the practice.

SELF-LOVE CHECKLIST

Because self-love can be so difficult to practice, it can be beneficial to set specific time aside for it. The following list provides some ideas on how to practice loving yourself. Space is provided to add additional self-love practices you enjoy to the list.

- ☐ Told myself "I'm proud of you"
- ☐ Planned one thing I'm looking forward to
- ☐ Took at least twenty minutes to myself
- ☐ Thanked my body for one thing it has helped me with
- ☐ Set a boundary
- ☐ Asked myself what I would say to a friend if they were in my situation
- ☐ Moved my body
- ☐ Reminded myself "I am doing the best I can in this moment"

- ☐ Took time to do a hobby I love
- ☐ Kept myself hydrated
- ☐ Talked to a friend about my feelings
- ☐ Other: _____
  _____
- ☐ Other: _____
  _____
- ☐ Other: _____
  _____

Have you practiced any of these acts of self-love this week? Aim to incorporate at least three each week. Check them off as you practice each one.

I am worthy of kindness
and compassion.

CARING FOR YOURSELF

So often when talking about the importance of self-love to deal with relationship anxiety with my clients, I hear, "But shouldn't I be putting energy into my partner over myself?" When things go wrong in a relationship, it is common to think about what you need to do for the other person, but sometimes what you need is to focus on your personal growth first.

How do you feel about paying attention to your own well-being even when you are in a relationship? What benefits do you see to self-care? How can your relationship benefit when you show yourself compassion and practice self-care?

SELF-CARE ACTION PLAN

How often have you thought about practicing self-care or doing something for yourself, but decided you don't have the time? Sometimes you just have to get started in order to incorporate it into your routine. Remember that self-care and prioritizing yourself can help you manage your relationship anxiety by building your capacity and improving your mood.

This exercise is designed to help you form a specific plan for your self-care practice. Plan four self-care strategies you will complete in the next week. Be as detailed as possible as you fill out the what, where and when, and preparation boxes.

WHAT	WHERE AND WHEN	PREPARATION
Example: Go out to watch a movie on my own	Movie theater on Thursday at 6 p.m.	I will ask my partner to stay home with the kids and I will buy the ticket on Monday.

A MONTH OF SELF-COMPLIMENTS

Complimenting yourself can be uncomfortable, but it has many benefits for building self-compassion. In the coming month, try to incorporate one compliment a day for yourself using this calendar. Even if you feel strange doing it at first, I encourage you to continue giving yourself praise throughout the month and assess how your feelings about doing so change.

	WEEK 1	WEEK 2	WEEK 3	WEEK 4
MON	I am creative	I am skilled	I look great	I am intelligent
TUE	I accept myself for who I am	I am kind	I am talented	I am a great _____ _____
WED	I am self-reflective	I am insightful	My body is strong	I am smart
THU	I am a positive addition to a team	I am thoughtful	I am driven	I am worthy of love
FRI	I am patient	I know what I am doing	I deserve rest	I am open-minded
SAT	I have been working really hard	I made someone feel special	I have grown	I am a hard worker
SUN	I would love to have a friend like me	I make people feel comfortable	I love fiercely	I am a good partner

POSITIVE SELF-TALK

Think about your closest friend or family member. Pretend they are going through the same relationship anxiety that you are and that they need someone to understand what they are going through. What would you say to them? Normally, we are so much more compassionate to others than to ourselves. Now read back the words you told your friend but address them to yourself. How do you feel? How is this different than how you normally speak to yourself?

SELF-LOVE STRETCH

Many people have difficulty with self-love when it comes to their bodies. Our bodies do so much for us, and taking time to thank and appreciate our bodies is an important self-love exercise. This exercise will assist you in developing a new appreciation for your body. Follow along with these stretching instructions and feel free to substitute phrases that resonate with you or with body parts you want to highlight.

1. Start stretching your neck by pulling it forward and rolling your head to the left and right. Stroke the sides of your neck and say to yourself, "I am thankful for my neck and head that allow me to have awareness and move to see in different directions."

2. Stretch each arm across your body and then over your head and say, "I am thankful for my arms that allow me to drive, eat, reach, type, and build."

3. Stretch your torso by reaching up and side to side and say, "I am thankful for my torso and stomach that holds everything that nourishes me and helps me sit, lift, and move my body."

4. Stretch your legs one at a time and say, "I am thankful for my strong legs that allow me to walk, exercise, sit, and go from place to place."

5. End with some deep breaths and by saying, "I am thankful for my body and all of its capabilities."

STANDING UP TO YOUR INNER CRITIC

We all have it: a voice inside the back of our mind that harshly judges what we do. When it comes to relationships, this inner critic can get in the way of believing we are worthy of finding joy with a partner.

One way to counter self-critical messages is by responding to them with the words of your inner nurturer—the compassionate part of yourself that knows you are worthy of love. How would your inner nurturer respond to the following statements? Write your answers in the spaces provided.

Statement: "I'm so embarrassed I said that. No wonder no one wants to be with me."

Response:

Statement: "Why can't I be a better partner? I know they're going to leave me this time."

Response:

Statement: "Why did I sleep with them? I bet they won't take me seriously now."

Response:

Statement: "I think I'll cancel. There's no way this will turn into a second date anyway."

Response: ....

....

....

Statement: "I'm trying so hard but it's still not working. I must try harder to make it work."

Response: ....

....

....

Statement: "If we break up, I'll be alone forever!"

Response: ....

....

....

POST-IT POWER

Sometimes we need to remind ourselves of the self-love we deserve. It is so easy to think negatively about ourselves. Unfortunately, we need to work hard to retrain our brains to see the positive sides of ourselves. Research has indicated that the average person thinks negative thoughts 80 percent of the time—and our thoughts impact our feelings deeply.

A good way to practice relearning how to think neutrally and incorporate positive thoughts about yourself is by building your exposure to more positive thoughts. One way to do this is to see them visually.

1. On Post-it Notes, write down some self-love phrases like "I love how kind you are" or "I am proud of how hard you are working on your mental health."

2. If this is difficult for you, think about what you might tell a friend.

3. Post these somewhere you will see them every day for a week, like your refrigerator or bathroom mirror, or even on your phone (you can set an alert to remind yourself to look at them, too).

4. If you wish, you can also say the phrases out loud to yourself for extra affirmation.

TELL A FRIEND

Because we are almost always harder on ourselves than we are on our friends, take some time to reflect and write down what you would tell a pal in each of these situations. Then apply it to yourself to build self-compassion.

What would you tell a friend who was in an unhealthy relationship?

....

....

....

What would you tell a friend who was feeling emotionally exhausted?

....

....

....

What would you tell a friend who hadn't practiced self-care in over a month?

....

....

....

What would you tell a friend who blamed themself for everything?

....

....

....

SELF-RESPECT CHECKLIST

When you respect yourself you are sending a message that you should also expect respect from others around you. Take some time to reflect on what self-respect means to you. The following list contains some ways to practice it. Put a check mark next to actions that resonate with you. Add other self-respect practices that work for you at the end of the list.

☐ Take time for self-care   ☐ Follow through

☐ Express yourself when you're hurt   ☐ Organize yourself

☐ Don't stay in toxic situations   ☐ Avoid putting yourself down

☐ Say no   ☐ Other: ....

☐ Set a boundary   ☐ Other: ....

☐ Say something loving to yourself   ☐ Other: ....

☐ Take a step toward a goal you have ☐ Other: ....

I can have empathy for myself the same way I would for a loved one.

Key Takeaways

After reading this chapter my hope is that you don't feel alone in your relationship anxiety. Building compassion for yourself can be a helpful tool in managing the stress of relationships. Creating self-love, self-compassion, and self-care strategies can lead you to rediscover love for yourself and help with personal growth before strengthening a relationship. Some key takeaways from this chapter are:

- Reframing negative thoughts to be more neutral and compassionate can minimize relationship anxiety.

- Practicing compassion for yourself by pretending you are a friend is a helpful empathy-building tool.

- Self-love can feel uncomfortable at first, but repetitive exposure to it can make it feel normal and valuable over time.

- Practicing self-respect teaches us that we should expect respect in our relationships.

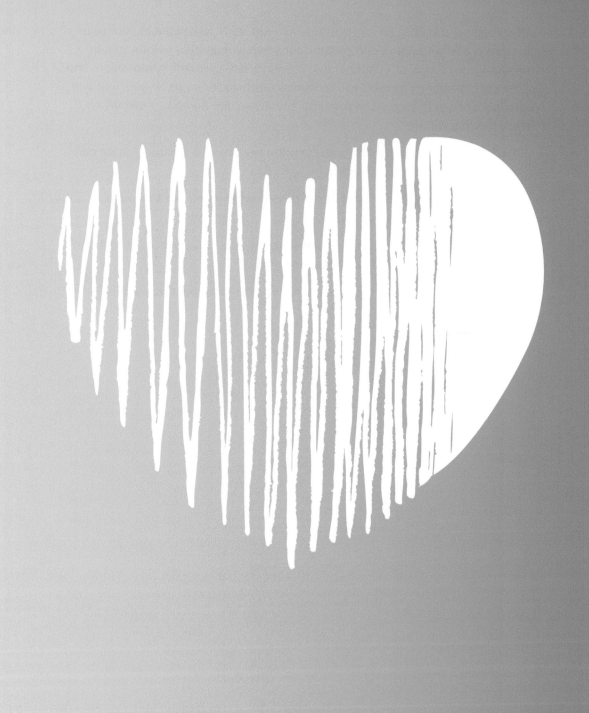

CHAPTER SIX

Rebuilding Your Self-Confidence

SELF-ESTEEM AND SELF-CONFIDENCE CAN BE INDICATORS OF relationship satisfaction. The more confident we are in ourselves, the less relationship anxiety we will likely have. You may struggle to feel confident in your relationship if you have a history of being invalidated during past unions, didn't have your needs met in childhood, or didn't see healthy relationships modeled growing up.

This chapter will focus on how to rebuild your self-confidence to minimize your anxiety and build a healthy relationship. The following pages include several exercises to help you build confidence in communicating your needs and wants, as well as resolve conflict in your relationships. These practices will encourage you to reflect on what you want in a relationship and how you are currently being treated by your partner. You will also be able to explore what specific situations in your relationship cause anxiety and build the confidence to address those issues with your partner.

CASE STUDY | **Marcus**

Marcus, who has been working with me in therapy for more than two years, has begun dating again after ending an emotionally abusive relationship where his partner would put him down and belittle him often. In his dating experiences he has noticed that he often can't tell if he likes someone or not because he is so concerned about whether they are interested in him. He feels his worries about ending up alone creep in during every date, and he often feels like people are "out of his league." For instance, he worries that the people he dates will be turned off by his career or the amount of money he makes.

Every time Marcus brought up dating, he would always focus on what he thought others were interested in instead of his own interests. He would say things like "I'm sure they weren't interested in me" or "I got a feeling they didn't think I was good enough for them."

After exploring why centering on his own needs in relationships was difficult, we discovered that Marcus's lack of self-confidence was severely impacting his ability to connect with his dates. Through exploration and exercises, Marcus realized that none of his dates were saying they didn't like him. Instead, Marcus's lack of self-confidence was getting in the way of building connection with them. After further processing and implementing many exercises to boost self-confidence, Marcus is able to express what he is looking for in a partner. Now he comes home from dates and writes down what he felt about the connection in an effort to focus on his needs and desires.

WHAT ARE YOUR STRENGTHS?

We all have personal strengths; sometimes we just don't take time to think about them and reflect on our positive characteristics. On the following list, check the strengths you possess, or write your own in the space provided.

☐ Dedicated   ☐ Motivated

☐ Determined   ☐ Organized

☐ Friendly   ☐ Patient

☐ Funny   ☐ Strong

☐ Generous   ☐ Thoughtful

☐ Genuine   ☐ Other: ....

☐ Good friend   ☐ Other: ....

☐ Kind   ☐ Other: ....

☐ Leader   ☐ Other: ....

☐ Loyal   ☐ Other: ....

My top five strengths are:

1. ....

2. ....

3. ....

4. ....

5. ....

BUILDING CONFIDENCE

Take a moment to describe how you have seen confidence demonstrated around you. What does confidence mean to you? What are some of the obstacles getting in the way of your being more confident? What do you think would help you build your self-confidence?

_____

_____

_____

_____

_____

_____

_____

_____

_____

_____

_____

_____

 I know myself better than anyone else, and I will make the right choices for myself.

HEALTHY VS. UNHEALTHY RELATIONSHIPS

It can be extremely helpful to have an awareness of how healthy or unhealthy your relationship is. Explore your most recent or current dating situation or relationship. Write down what was or is *healthy* about your relationship in the left column. Then write what was or is *unhealthy* about your relationship in the right column.

Note: There may be parts of a relationship that can be unhealthy and something you and your partner are working on without being a completely unhealthy relationship. Try to be honest during this exercise. No one but you will see it.

HEALTHY	UNHEALTHY
Example: We try to communicate when we are upset.	I sometimes raise my voice when I'm trying to communicate.

ANXIETY VS. INTUITION

It is common for people to have difficulty identifying anxiety versus intuition because they sometimes feel similar. I often hear my clients say, "How do I know if it's a gut feeling or anxiety when I always feel like something bad is going to happen?" If you feel similarly, it might be helpful to think about how these feelings are different.

- **Anxiety** is focused on worries or fears about a particular situation. It often includes physical symptoms such as increased heart rate or feeling restless, tired, or nauseous.

- **Intuition** is an immediate feeling and natural ability you have to know something about a situation without proof.

The difference in the two can be assessed by focusing on our feeling. Anxiety often feels stressful or intense, is future focused, and can involve strong physical symptoms, while intuition has a sense of calm to it, is focused on the present, and often comes after a period of reflection. For example, you may feel anxious after an argument with your partner because you are worrying about breaking up and have difficulty sleeping. Or, after having several arguments with your partner, you have an overwhelming feeling that tells you this is a relationship you no longer want to be in and you are confident about the conclusion. In this example, the anxiety is about the future, while the intuition comes after reflection.

Sometimes it is difficult to identify the difference between the two. When that happens, use the checklist on the following page. Whichever column has more check marks is most likely what you are experiencing.

ANXIETY	INTUITION
☐ Feel worried or fearful	☐ Physical response in your stomach
☐ Feel physically nauseous	☐ Feel a sense of calm or certainty
☐ Feel restless	☐ Feeling comes after reflection
☐ Focused on things in the future	☐ Focused on something happening in the present moment
☐ Increased heart rate	☐ Sense of certainty in your decision or thoughts

DOES YOUR PARTNER AFFECT YOUR CONFIDENCE?

While self-confidence is essential in a relationship, it will only go so far if you aren't supported by a caring and compassionate partner. A healthy relationship is a two-way street in which you recognize each other's positive qualities and encourage each other to become your best selves.

Take this quiz to see if your partner is nurturing your self-confidence or not. Circle yes or no for each question.

1. Your partner makes important decisions without you. **YES | NO**

2. Your partner is not body positive. **YES | NO**

3. You feel that you are constantly apologizing to your partner. **YES | NO**

4. Your partner does not respect your time with family and friends. **YES | NO**

5. Your partner mocks you. **YES | NO**

6. Your partner often rechecks or redoes the things you just did. **YES | NO**

7. Your partner constantly questions your choices. **YES | NO**

8. Your partner takes over things you were doing. **YES | NO**

If you circled "yes" in four or more boxes, it is possible that your partner is affecting your confidence. It is normal for you to feel down or for your confidence to be impacted if your partner is treating you unkindly or making you feel unsupported. If this resonates, you may consider talking to your partner about your current journey toward building self-confidence.

You can also list specific ways they could help you build your confidence. For example, say, "I really appreciate praise and words of affirmation. If there are times you feel appreciative of me, I would really like to hear that." Chapter seven of this workbook (page 103) can give you more strategies for communicating with your partner. You can also process this further with a therapist or by using the Resources section at the end of this workbook (page 137).

If you feel unsafe discussing this with your partner or feel that you are in an abusive or controlling relationship, please seek support outside this workbook with a therapist or loved one, or by calling the domestic violence hotline at 800-799-7233.

SUPERHERO POSE

Believe it or not, posing like a superhero with your arms in the air or with two arms on your waist for two minutes helps boost your mood, increase confidence, and improve self-esteem. This pose has even been shown to lower levels of cortisol, which is the body's stress hormone. Take some time to practice a superhero pose and minimize anxiety by following the directions here.

1. Take five big deep breaths in through the nose and slowly out through the mouth.

2. Stand up and commit to a superhero pose.

3. As you are standing in your superhero pose, continue your breathing.

4. Hold this position for two minutes.

5. Check in with yourself to see if you are feeling less anxious or stressed afterward.

 I am confident in my ability to build
healthy relationships.

MY IDEAL PARTNER

We have all daydreamed about our perfect partner: what they would look like and how they would treat us. Take your manifesting a step further by writing out the characteristics of your ideal partner here. Think about how you want them to treat you and how you want to be able to deal with any conflicts that arise.

_____

_____

_____

_____

_____

After reflecting on your ideal partner, take some time to think about three non-negotiable characteristics your future or current partner must have and write them down here. An example of a nonnegotiable is feeling safe or comfortable with them. By adding this to your list you would be saying that this is something you are not willing to negotiate. These should be of the utmost importance to you in a relationship. Keep this list handy while dating to make sure any potential partners are meeting your nonnegotiable list.

1. _____

_____

2. _____

_____

3. _____

_____

REFLECTING ON YOUR RELATIONSHIPS

Let's dig a little deeper and think about a situation where you were experiencing relationship anxiety. Write about the details. How did you handle the situation? What improvements could you have made? Describe the skills and communication strategies you can use to minimize your anxiety.

Now, take a moment to reflect on what a healthy relationship means to you. What characteristics are part of a healthy relationship? Are you currently in one? Are there things you can improve in your relationship to make it healthier? How would you communicate this to your partner?

HALF SMILE

It can be hard to remain in a good mood or emotionally regulated when we are talking about unhealthy relationships or difficult conversations. Half smile is a strategy you can use to remain emotionally regulated during difficult times.

Practice half smile by beginning to smile with your lips and stopping when the corners of your mouth have been slightly turned up like a tiny smile. You can try this when you are on the phone with someone who triggers you or when you are feeling frustrated. Practicing half smile for five to ten minutes will have an immediate effect on your mood, leading you to feel happier.

Our physical bodies are so strongly connected to our emotions that when we practice this technique, we experience the same happiness we would feel if we were genuinely smiling. Give this a try the next time you are feeling anxious, overwhelmed, or frustrated.

STAYING IN THE PRESENT

Thinking about hard conversations and conflict can lead to a spiral of anxious thoughts and behaviors. Consistently practicing mindfulness is a strong coping strategy for minimizing stress. Take a moment to practice this activity to build your focus on the present.

1. Take several deep breaths in through the nose and out through the mouth.

2. Ask yourself, "What is in front of me?" and answer.

3. Ask yourself, "What do you need in this moment?" and answer.

4. Ground yourself by saying "In this moment I am safe."

5. As anxious thoughts come to mind, acknowledge them and then watch them float away, bringing yourself back to the here and now by asking yourself, "What is in front of me?" again.

WHAT WOULD YOU SAY?

You are now equipped with many strategies to have difficult conversations and build your confidence. Let's imagine that you need to communicate with your partner about your relationship anxiety and that there are no consequences to the words you use with them. Use this exercise to practice what you are hoping to say to your partner as you build confidence. Fill in the blanks with your answers.

The thing I need from you is:

....

....

I want you to:

....

....

The thing I love about you is:

....

....

The thing I can't wait to do with you is:

....

....

I want you to know this about me:

....

....

VISUALIZING YOUR FUTURE

You may have heard the phrase "seeing is believing." Visualization is a tool that can help you imagine different situations and see and feel yourself accomplishing something that is important to you.

In this case, visualizing yourself in a healthy relationship can help you gain confidence, boost motivation, and decrease the anxiety involved in making it a reality. When you see yourself in a healthy relationship through visualization it is easier to believe having it will be possible.

1. Find a comfortable position seated or lying down.

2. Take some deep, gentle breaths in and out to ground yourself.

3. Close your eyes and imagine yourself one year from today. Envisage yourself with a year of building skills under your belt and feeling prepared to be in a healthy relationship.

4. Reflect on what you see. Who do you envision yourself with? What does a healthy relationship look like? How are your needs met?

5. Envision the happiness and the feeling of pride you have in yourself for working on this goal.

Key Takeaways

In this chapter we discussed how to build your self-confidence and trust in yourself. We discussed how lack of self confidence can negatively affect relationships. This chapter introduced some exercises to improve self-confidence. You were able to reflect on past and current relationships to identify if they were/are healthy or not, and you practiced strategies to be able to effectively express yourself. Most important, this chapter allowed you to reflect on your feelings about your current relationship and how it impacts you. Some key takeaways from this chapter include:

- Our physical and emotional health are intertwined.

- Just because there is an unhealthy part of a relationship, this does not necessarily mean the entire relationship is unhealthy.

- Our partners can impact our self-confidence.

- Reflecting on your needs and wants for a relationship in writing can be particularly helpful.

CHAPTER SEVEN

Knowing Your Boundaries and Communicating Your Needs

NOW THAT YOU HAVE WORKED ON REBUILDING YOUR self-confidence, the next step to minimize your relationship anxiety is to work on communicating your needs. Communication and expressing your emotions can feel daunting. Many people worry that doing so will cause their partner to run away or think poorly of them, when in reality, the more we communicate the more connection we build.

At any stage of a relationship—whether you are swiping on apps, dating, or in a long-term relationship—communication and boundary setting are important. The exercises in this chapter will assist you in building your communication skills, as well as help you reflect on your relationship history and what healthy boundaries are important for you in the future.

In this chapter, you will not only reflect on your communication skills but also build listening and validation skills so that your partner feels heard, too. After this type of reflection, questions about your relationship and if you want to continue in it may come up for you. This chapter will also help you reflect on relationships you want to end and how to process and work through breakups.

CASE STUDY | **Jennifer**

Jennifer had been swiping on dating apps and was constantly worried about the expectations of people she met. Some of the worries running through her head were: "Will they be disappointed in me? Will they pressure me to have sex? Will they ghost me after one date?" Jennifer had been on the apps for about a year and felt put off by some of her experiences and sad that her dates never went as hoped or expected.

With the help of her therapist, Jennifer discovered that she had never put thought into what she wanted in a partner and had not taken time to think about important boundaries within relationships. By exploring her feelings, she discovered that she may not have an issue with dating, but more with her communication and boundary setting within relationships. Jennifer took time to reflect on what she wanted in a partner and what she wanted out of dating. She decided that the most important things for her were building connection, having a committed relationship, and finding someone who makes her laugh.

With the help of some friends, Jennifer restructured her dating profiles to include that she was interested in a committed relationship and that humor was important to her. She began to spend less time talking on the app and was more straightforward about wanting to meet to see if there was a connection. Since being more honest with herself and others about her needs, she was able to set boundaries when she met someone who was not what she was looking for by saying "Sounds like this isn't a match" or "This isn't what I'm looking for." Setting boundaries and using communication has made dating feel more manageable for Jennifer.

HONEST COMMUNICATION

Communicating honestly can be intimidating for many because of the vulnerability it requires. We all have thoughts and feelings we keep to ourselves and don't like to share. When the avoidance of communication between us and our partners grows, we create distance in the relationship. Remember that you have built many skills to work through some of these difficult feelings and you are capable of communicating your needs.

Take a moment to reflect on why communication has been difficult for you. Write down why it is important for your relationship. If you could express your feelings to your partner honestly without consequences, what would you say?

GUIDELINES FOR EFFECTIVE COMMUNICATION

Sometimes we just don't know where to start when it comes to communication. You may have things you want to communicate to your partner but worry about how they will be interpreted or feel like you don't know how to express yourself clearly. The following guidelines were adapted from the dialectical behavior therapy (DBT) model and provide a starting point to practice communication. Review the guidelines and try to have one conversation this week using this DEAR strategy.

Describe the situation and stick to the facts. *Example: "You told me you would be free on Saturday for our plans, and now you're telling me you won't be."*

Express your feelings about the situation using I statements. *Example: "I feel like I am not a priority when you do this."*

Ask for what you want. *Example: "When you make plans with me, I need you to stick to them."*

Reward the person by explaining the positive effects of getting what you need. *Example: "This would really help make our relationship stronger and stop us from arguing so much."*

 I am capable of communicating my needs. I know that my needs are important and valid.

FEELING OPPOSITE EMOTIONS

I often hear from family, friends, and clients that they sometimes feel "over-whelmed" or "crazy" because they are experiencing opposite emotions at the same time within their relationship. If you feel this way, I assure you that this is a typical feeling. Much like when people express love and hate in relationships, there are often opposite feelings that happen in relationships and dating.

Another word for balancing these two opposite emotions happening in the same moment is dialectics. Dialectics validate that opposite feelings can occur at the same time. Knowing this can be beneficial because it helps self-validate your feelings and minimize confusion during stressful moments. It also helps us eliminate anxious thoughts such as "We're in an argument, so this must be over." Instead, we can shift to validating all the feelings happening in the situation by saying "I'm frustrated with my partner, and I know we will work through this." Following are common dialectics we feel in relationships. Check the ones you have felt in relationships or dating.

- [ ] I want to be an independent person, and I also enjoy being close to someone.

- [ ] I want to prioritize myself and the relationship.

- [ ] I know I can trust my partner, and sometimes I worry that they will cheat on me.

- [ ] I want to improve myself, and I am doing the best I can right now.

- [ ] I want to be alone a lot of the time, and I want to feel connected to my partner.

- [ ] I want to share my deep feelings and also keep things to myself.

- [ ] I understand why my partner acts out, and I can ask them to change their behavior.

- [ ] I can be upset with someone and respect them.

REFLECTIVE LISTENING

Communication is only one side of the equation. While it is important that you can express yourself clearly in relationships, it is also crucial to make your partner feel listened to when they are communicating, too. When we make our partners feel listened to, they are more likely to listen to us. Here are some guidelines for reflective listening. Try these the next time you and your partner are communicating.

- Give your full attention by putting away or turning off distractions like your TV, phone, and computer. Focus only on the person speaking.

- Show your interest by making eye contact, nodding your head, facing your body toward the person, and sitting next to them.

- Rephrase and confirm what they are saying to ensure you are under- standing them. You might start by saying, "So you feel . . . is that right?" or "I want to make sure I understand, you're saying . . ."

- Validate the feelings even if you disagree with the content. This helps your partner feel understood and builds closeness in the relationship. You might validate your partner with one of the following statements:

  "I can understand why you felt that way."

  "You have been going through a lot lately."

  "I'm so sorry you've been going through this."

HOW TO ASK OPEN-ENDED QUESTIONS

Asking open-ended questions is a helpful way to learn about your partner and connect on a deeper level. Open-ended questions can provide you with more detail and information as well as show your partner that you are interested in learning about their perspective and experiences. You can start asking effective open-ended questions by starting with *how*, *why*, *what*, *describe*, or *tell me*.

When we are upset with our partners, it is common to speak in an accusatory manner or ask yes or no questions. This often creates more tension and distance in the relationship, making it more difficult to repair the current situation. Instead of asking "Do you even like me?" say, "How are you feeling about me and this relationship?" Instead of saying "I don't even know if you care about me," try saying, "Sometimes I'm unsure how you feel about me. Can you tell me?" These minor changes can help you slow down and focus on the facts.

Brainstorm some open-ended questions that would help you connect with your partner.

1. ....
....
....
....

2. ....
....
....
....

3. ....
....
....
....

YOUR BOUNDARIES

Let's talk about relationship boundaries, which help you define and express what you are comfortable with and how you would like to be treated. Boundaries might sound like "Even if you are upset, please don't raise your voice" or "I need space to hang out with friends and enjoy things on my own." It can be helpful to think through boundaries that are important to you no matter what your relationship status is.

You can have physical, emotional, sexual, intellectual, or financial boundaries in your relationship. What boundaries are important to you? Have you been able to set these in your current or in a previous relationship?

....

....

....

....

....

Do boundaries come easy to you, or are they difficult to communicate? What gets in the way of setting them? What boundaries would you like to express to your current or future partner?

....

....

....

....

....

CHECKING IN WITH EACH OTHER

Relationship anxiety is often exacerbated when we feel distance between ourselves and our partner. One way to work toward building connection instead of distance is to schedule a weekly time to check in about your schedule, feelings, and needs, as well as to simply connect and communicate. This time can be as official or unofficial as you'd like. It can be over dinner, in the car, or on the couch after watching a movie.

Connection is always easier when we add praise and validation. Be sure to include tokens of love and appreciation in this weekly meeting; this might sound like "I want to start by saying I really notice the support you've been giving me and I appreciate it."

Use this table to organize your thoughts and keep yourself accountable for meeting with your partner over the next four weeks. Check the final row when you have completed each week's plan.

	WEEK 1	WEEK 2	WEEK 3	WEEK 4
Where and when				
I want to discuss . . .				
How to show love or appreciation				
Completed?				

PROS AND CONS

Exploring communication with your partner and reflecting on your boundaries can lead to questions about whether this is a relationship you want to continue to be in. It is healthy to have this type of reflection. If the relationship has red flags that you need to explore, it can be productive to create a pros and cons list in the table provided.

Note: This exercise is not for relationships that are emotionally or physically abusive. If you feel that your relationship is abusive, please call the National Domestic Violence Hotline at 800-799-7233 and/or see the Resources (page 137) for more tools and information.

PROS TO STAYING IN RELATIONSHIP	CONS TO STAYING IN RELATIONSHIP

If you have decided this is a relationship you would like to work through from the pros and cons list, use DEAR (page 106) to express your feelings about working on the relationship:

Describe the situation and stick to the facts:

....

....

Express your feelings about the situation:

....

....

Ask for what you want:

....

....

Reward your partner by explaining the positive effects of getting what you need:

....

....

MINDFULNESS WITH WILLING HANDS

We are constantly holding on to so much stress and anxiety. It can be overwhelming to go through life with this amount of tension in our bodies. When we feel overwhelmed in our personal lives, our relationships often suffer, too. It is important to take time for yourself to relieve stress. One way to do this is by adding willing hands to your mindfulness practice. The simple act of opening your hands can make it easier to release tension, frustration, and emotion from your body. To practice willing hands, follow these steps.

- Place your hands on your lap and thighs, with your hands unclenched and facing upward with open palms.

- Sit with your eyes closed and hands on your lap.

- Take a deep breath and focus on your breathing.

- Envision yourself breathing in clarity and breathing out frustration.

- Imagine yourself accepting peace in through your hands and releasing tension out through your hands.

- Continue this practice for five minutes. Reflect on your willingness to let go and to find inner peace.

COPING AHEAD

If you are in a place where you are feeling like you no longer want to be in your current relationship, it can be helpful to process your feelings by coping ahead. Thinking through the emotions you might feel during a breakup and what you will do and say can reduce stress ahead of time. To cope ahead, we want to imagine the situation as vividly as possible. Take a moment to imagine what a breakup would look like. What would you say? How would they react? What are different situations that might happen? What coping skills could you use to get through each possibility? Who could be supportive of you? What could you do after the breakup to soothe yourself?

BREAKUP SCRIPTS

Ending a relationship can be daunting. Many of my clients describe anxiety coming from thoughts about the actual breakup, as well as worries about what they will say or worries about how their partner will react. Finding the right words can be challenging. Just like in all forms of communication, being direct and clear are the most important parts of communication in a breakup. The following are some scripts for ending a relationship that may be helpful.

- This is difficult for me to say. I am not happy in this relationship. I don't feel that this relationship is healthy anymore and I want to break up.

- I have been thinking about our relationship a lot and have been feeling like we are not compatible because . . . I think it is best to move on and not see each other anymore.

- This is not working for me anymore. I don't feel we are on the same page, and I don't want to continue in this relationship.

- I really respect you and care about you, and I also do not think being with you is right for me. I don't think we should talk anymore.

Do any of those speak to your situation? You can use the space provided to adapt one or more of these to make it more specific to what you want to say, or create an entirely different one. Remember, the key is to be direct and clear.

REGULATE WITH COLD WATER

Research indicates that cold water immersion increases mood elevating hormones, as well as alertness, clarity, and energy levels. One way to use the benefits of cold water for mental health is by submerging your face in cold water or covering it with a cold compress. This process can help with regulating your emotions by slowing down you heart rate and directing blood flow to your brain and heart, which can minimize distress in the moment. This could be a helpful coping skill you use during conflict or after a breakup. Follow these instructions to practice regulating with cold water.

1. Get a large bowl of cold water and fill it with ice.

2. Set a timer for ten to twenty seconds.

3. Holding your breath, gently dip your face in the bowl of water until the timer goes off.

4. Notice if this has helped you regulate your emotions.

 It is my time to put myself first. I have the coping skills to do hard things.

OPPOSITE ACTION

Relationships can be confusing at times. It is common to get overwhelmed with our feelings—like our brain is telling us one thing when our emotions are telling us something different. For example, we might feel like we love someone deeply but also know they are not healthy for us. One way to work through strong emotions is to act opposite of them.

For example, you may be feeling jealousy in the relationship. To act opposite of that emotion would include not snooping or looking through your partner's phone, not avoiding but instead confronting your worries by talking to your partner and working on feeling calm instead of angry by using deep breathing and mindfulness. While this strategy may seem challenging, it is often helpful to change your emotional reaction during difficult moments.

In the following table, list the action you are wanting to do based on how you are feeling and then how you could act opposite to better cope with the strong emotions.

EMOTION	RELATED URGE	OPPOSITE ACTION
Example: I feel sad about leaving my partner, even though I know it was the right thing to do.	To call them even though we said we wouldn't make contact for a long time.	Call up a friend instead and tell them how I'm feeling.

Key Takeaways

This chapter has highlighted the importance of communication and boundaries in a relationship. Through completing the exercises in this chapter, you have learned several communication strategies and skills to build connection with your partner and manage relationship anxiety. You have been able to reflect on your relationship and use effective communication to express your needs. Some of this reflection has led you to explore whether you are happy with your partner. If you have learned that you want to end a relationship, we have reviewed strategies you can use in a breakup. Some key takeaways from this chapter include:

- Listening to your partner is equally important for communicating effectively with them.

- Validating each other can improve your relationship and build closeness.

- It is common to feel two opposite emotions in one instance.

- Communicating boundaries helps each partner learn about the other.

- Coping ahead is a powerful strategy to regulate emotions and prepare for the future.

CHAPTER EIGHT

Reclaiming Your Joy in Relationships

TAKE A MOMENT TO PAUSE AND BE PROUD OF YOURSELF FOR THE
deep exploration and practice you have put into working on
your relationship anxiety. It is not easy to reflect and process,
and you have been doing a lot of that. Now that you can identify
your emotions and triggers, practice self-compassion, and use
communication skills, it is time to allow yourself to reclaim joy in
your relationships.

Whether you are taking time for yourself, beginning to start
dating, or nourishing a long-term relationship, feeling joy is
crucial. I want to be clear: It is absolutely reasonable to not feel joy
all the time in your relationship, but being able to identify what
does bring you happiness can help you build connection with
your partner and relieve anxiety.

This chapter is about homing in on what brings you joy
in relationships and reflecting on what you want in all your
partnerships, both in the present and the future. This chapter
will also focus on bringing everything you have learned
together to confront your anxieties, reflect, and use the tools you
have worked on so you can move forward and build strong,
healthy relationships.

CASE STUDY | **Linda and Carla**

Linda and Carla have been close friends for several years. They are meeting for dinner, and Carla begins to express that she has been having relationship anxiety about a new guy she's been dating. Carla explains, "Things were going well, but I'm getting in my head about it. It's like I won't let myself be happy. I'm always waiting for the other shoe to drop."

Linda validates her friend and says, "I've been there; relationship anxiety is no joke. There was a time I just avoided my husband altogether because I was so worried I would find out he was doing something behind my back, even though nothing was going on."

Linda talked about some of the strategies that were most helpful for her and discussed how processing her triggers and communicating in dating might be helpful for Carla. After reflecting, Carla decided she needed to do some processing. With more awareness of her triggers and emotions—and by practicing self-compassion—she has been able to be direct and communicate effectively while dating. She has been able to ask questions instead of avoiding her partner, which has helped her develop a stronger relationship and allowed her to experience joy in a bond for the first time.

FEELING CALM AND CONTENT WITH BREATH WORK

We have practiced deep breathing together in past chapters. In this exercise we are focusing on a combination of breathing exercises. Practicing our breath work and connecting with our breath can help develop a sense of calm, happiness, and self-awareness. In this exercise, let's set an intention to cultivate joy. As you follow the steps, be open to feelings of happiness.

1. Find a comfortable position, allow your body to settle, and close your eyes.

2. Bring awareness to your breath and notice your breaths coming in and going out.

3. Set an intention by telling yourself, "I deserve to experience joy."

4. Feel the breath passing in through your nostrils and out through your lips. Continue to focus on your breaths in and out.

5. Notice your body relax as you breathe in through your nose and out through your mouth.

6. As you continue to breathe in and out, notice the turning point where the in-breath becomes the out-breath. Notice the rhythm of your breath.

7. As you continue to inhale and exhale, feel yourself fill with joy with each inhale. Say to yourself "I allow in joy" as you inhale.

8. With each exhale, feel your body release your anxieties and worries.

9. Continue for ten to fifteen breaths.

10. When you are ready, gently open your eyes and bring your awareness back to the present.

REMEMBERING HAPPINESS

It can be difficult to feel joy in relationships when we are working through our anxieties or problems. Incorporating joy into our relationships must be intentional. Sometimes it is just a matter of remembering what it felt like and that it is possible to feel that again. Think about a time you felt happiness in a relationship or in your personal life. Why is it important to feel this in your relationship? What specific things bring you joy in your relationship? What can your partner do to bring you joy? How can you bring joy to your partner? Feel free to include your partner in this reflection.

MANIFESTING JOY

Manifestation is a concept of attracting things into your life through believing they are possible and visualizing yourself achieving them. This is the first step toward fostering joy in your relationship. If you have experienced trauma in partnerships before, it can be difficult to even imagine yourself in a joyful and healthy relationship, and this may be something that you need to process further. If it feels right for you, let's take time to explore.

1. Start by telling yourself you will feel joy in your relationship.

2. Close your eyes and envision yourself with a smile on your face. Imagine yourself with minimal worries and anxieties.

3. Try to picture yourself and your partner in a happy place where both of you are free of worry.

4. Notice what you are doing that is bringing you joy in the picture in your mind. How does it feel?

5. Reflect on what differences you notice between the self you envision and yourself now.

6. Tell yourself that it is possible to feel that same joy. Tell yourself that you will get there.

MY IDEAL RELATIONSHIP

Let's talk about your ideal relationship. Even if you are currently in a relationship, it can be helpful to think through the qualities that are important to you in
a healthy union. Reflect on the characteristics that you value in a partner and in
yourself. What are some of the qualities of your ideal partner? How do they act
around you? What kind of communicator are they? How do you act in your ideal
relationship? What traits do you show? Within the figures drawn on this page
label the qualities you and your partner have in your ideal relationship. When
you are finished, reflect on what areas show your strengths and what you need
to improve on.

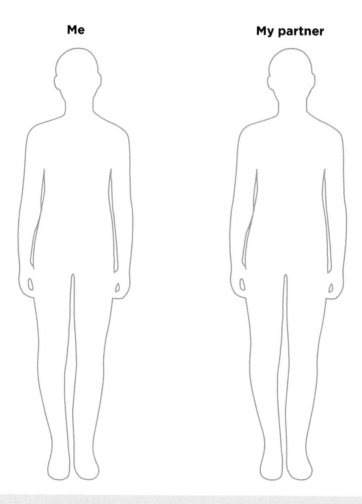

Me **My partner**

A MONTH OF JOY

Creating joy in your relationship has to be intentional sometimes. The more time we set aside to build our happiness, the more likely it is to fill our relationship. Follow this calendar for ideas you can use every day for the next month to incorporate joy into your daily life.

	WEEK 1	WEEK 2	WEEK 3	WEEK 4
MON	Take a photo of something that brings joy	Tell yourself "I am worthy of feeling joy."	Eat your favorite meal or dessert	Tell yourself "I will feel joy."
TUE	Reframe a worry in a more neutral way	Tell a joke	Plan a date with your partner	Give your partner a thirty-second hug
WED	Write a thank-you note	Schedule a self-care day	Do an act of kindness for your partner	Spend time outside
THU	Write down three things you're thankful for	Hug a friend	Create an uplifting playlist	Practice your half smile (page 97)
FRI	Find joy in music, singing, or dancing	Watch your favorite movie	Ask your partner what makes them happy	Get dressed up
SAT	Smile at a stranger	Share a happy memory with someone	Say something nice to yourself	Organize something in your home
SUN	Start a list of things that bring joy	Move your body	Visualize yourself happy	Tell your partner one thing they do that brings you joy

EXPRESSING GRATITUDE

One way to build joy is through gratitude. It can be challenging to feel grateful when we are in a difficult place emotionally. When we feel anxious or depressed it is hard to see outside that. Yet setting daily time to reflect on gratitude has been proven to improve mental health and relationships. When we have appreciation for meaningful aspects of our life, our overall health improves, and we experience less stress. Taking time to express gratitude helps us find balance when we are overwhelmed with anxiety. Complete this exercise as a reflection of what you are grateful for.

Write down three things you are grateful for in general:

1. ....

2. ....

3. ....

Now write down three things you are grateful for about dating or in your relationship:

1. ....

2. ....

3. ....

Now write down three things you are grateful for about a particular dating experience or in your current relationship:

1. ....

2. ....

3. ....

VISION BOARD

A vision board is a collage of images and words that align with your hopes, values, and goals, created as a reminder and for motivation. A vision board can be helpful in reclaiming the joy in your relationship and can help you see that it is possible to feel happiness. Think about what you want for yourself and your relationship, as well as which experiences and situations would create joy for you. Follow these directions to create a vision board.

- Gather supplies for your vision board, such as paper, glue, tape, scissors, magazines, markers, etc.

- In preparation for creating a vision board, write down everything you can think of that represents joy in relationships for you.

- Use images, words, and/or drawings as an art form to represent your wishes for yourself when it comes to joy in relationships.

Once completed, put the vision board somewhere you can see it as a reminder that you are worthy of joy and capable of feeling it.

 I know that I will feel joy in relationships again.

BRINGING IT ALL TOGETHER

We have covered many skills throughout this workbook to help you manage your relationship anxiety and build healthy partnerships. Take a moment to think about a situation that has recently sparked relationship anxiety for you. Use the skills from each chapter to process the situation and develop a solution.

Write down a situation in which you felt relationship anxiety:

Identify emotions you felt:

Identify possible triggers:

How did you practice self-compassion?

What could you tell yourself to rebuild your confidence?

List communication strategies that are helpful in this situation:

What was the result of using these skills? Now that you have processed this situation, how did you reclaim joy in it?

REFLECTING ON YOUR NEW SKILLS

In part 2 of this workbook, each chapter has focused on different skills to help you minimize your relationship anxiety. How are you currently using—or planning to use—the skills you've learned?

....

....

....

How do you hope that these skills will impact your relationship anxiety?

....

....

....

Now think in particular about which tools you will use when you experience strong feelings of anxiety in difficult situations. List three skills that you can use when you need to regulate your emotions.

1. ....

2. ....

3. ....

I am confident that the
skills I have learned can ease
my relationship anxiety.

EMBRACING DIFFERENCES AND SIMILARITIES

We all have different things that bring us joy. It is common for people in a relationship to have diverse sources of joy. Sometimes you may feel discouraged if there are disparities between what brings you joy versus what brings your partner joy. Visually representing our differences and similarities can help highlight how we can connect with our partners.

Reflect on what brings you joy and write it on the "me" section of the Venn diagram. Reflect on what brings your partner joy, or if you feel comfortable, invite them in to describe some of the things that bring them joy and write these under the "my partner" part of the diagram. Are there things that overlap? Then write them in the "both" section. If they don't intersect, have a discussion with your partner about things you both enjoy that you could do together.

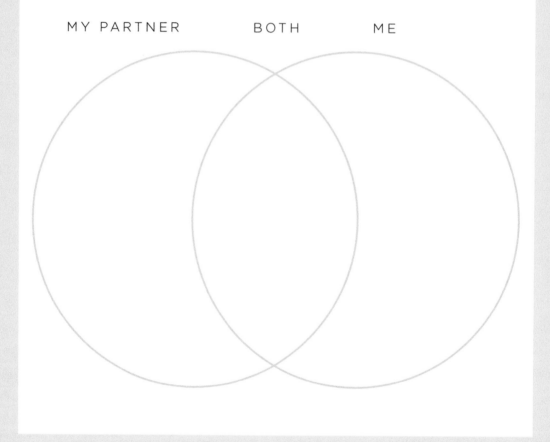

MY PARTNER   BOTH   ME

FILL IN THE BLANK

Now that this workbook is coming to an end, it is important to bring all the skills you have learned together. The goal is to put you in touch with yourself and your needs so that you are able to work through relationship anxiety as it comes up and communicate your needs effectively. You are so capable of doing this! We know that even the most emotionally aware people with the largest toolboxes still experience anxiety from time to time. If you continue to experience relationship anxiety, I want you to be prepared with a plan. Fill in the blanks provided. I encourage you to share your results with your current or future partner so that you have a teammate in working toward alleviating your relationship anxiety.

Common triggers for my relationship anxiety are:

When I feel relationship anxiety, I will:

When I feel relationship anxiety, I would like my partner to:

The following coping strategies are helpful for me when I experience relationship anxiety:

Some useful phrases to help myself through my anxiety are:

Key Takeaways

Reclaiming your joy in relationships is the final step in addressing anxiety in your union. By focusing on joy, you can free yourself from tension and worries and instead focus on building a healthy relationship. In this chapter, we have explored how to put all the workbook skills together to minimize relationship anxiety. We have also worked on future tools to maintain the progress you've made and outline a plan if your relationship anxiety comes up again. Some key takeaways from this chapter are:

- Coping strategies are an integral part of healing from anxiety.

- Manifesting can help us foster joy in relationships.

- Incorporating joy in relationships often has to be intentional.

- You can build joy through gratitude.

- It is normal if you experience relationship anxiety again in the future.

A Final Note

Congratulations on completing the *Anxiety in Relationships Workbook*! It is not easy to reflect on yourself in such a deep way as you have. My hope is that you see your efforts, reflection, and practice pay off and that you have experienced improvements in your relationship anxiety already. Sometimes improvement takes time, and you may need to keep on reviewing some of the skills if you continue to feel anxious.

By now you understand that relationship anxiety is common but also something that can be managed with self-discovery and communication. Through addressing your relationship anxieties, understanding them, communicating them, and loving yourself, peace and acceptance are possible.

Take a moment to think back on your feelings when starting this workbook and notice the differences in how you felt then and how you feel now. I hope that you have gained the confidence to address the anxieties in your relationship and that you continue to always self-reflect and discover.

Relationships can be some of the most rewarding human experiences, and every person deserves to feel the happiness that comes from building connection. I hope that the skills you have learned in this workbook will bring you emotional health, happiness, and peace.

Resources

FINDING A THERAPIST OR SUPPORT GROUP
National Alliance on Mental Illness: Nami.org for mental health resources and support groups

Open Path Collective: Openpathcollective.org for affordable therapy

Psychology Today: Psychologytoday.com to find a therapist near you

FURTHER READING ABOUT RELATIONSHIPS AND ANXIETY
Attached by Amir Levine and Rachel Heller (a book on attachment styles)

Mind Over Mood workbook by Dennis Greenberger and Christine A. Padesky (a workbook on managing anxious thoughts)

MEDITATION TOOLS
Try the Calm app or the Headspace app for guided meditations. Free meditations can also be found on streaming services like YouTube and Spotify.

ASSISTANCE FOR VICTIMS OF ABUSE
Crisis Text Line: Text NAMI to 741-741

National Domestic Violence Hotline: 800-799-SAFE

National Sexual Assault Hotline: 800-656-HOPE

Thehotline.org for domestic violence information

FURTHER READING FOR HEALING FROM UNHEALTHY RELATIONSHIPS
The Emotional Abuse Recovery Workbook by Theresa Comito

The Gaslighting Recovery Workbook by Amy Marlow-Macoy

The Narcissism Recovery Workbook by Brenda Stephens

References

Beck, Judith S. *Cognitive Behavior Therapy: Basics and Beyond*. New York: The Guilford Press, 2021.

Greenberger, Dennis, and Christine A. Padesky. *Mind Over Mood: Change How You Feel by Changing the Way You Think*. New York: The Guilford Press, 2016.

Levine, Amir, and Rachel S. F. Heller. *Attached*. New York: TarcherPerigree, 2011.

Linehan, Marsha M. *DBT Skills Training Handouts and Worksheets, Second Edition*. New York: The Guilford Press, 2014.

National Alliance on Mental Illness. "Anxiety Disorders." Last modified December 2017. nami.org/About-Mental-Illness/Mental-Health-Conditions/Anxiety-Disorders.

Smyth, Joshua M., Jillian A. Johnson, Brandon J. Auer, Erik Lehman, Giampaolo Talamo, and Christopher N. Sciamanna. "Online Positive Affect Journaling in the Improvement of Mental Distress and Well-Being in General Medical Patients with Elevated Anxiety Symptoms: A Preliminary Randomized Controlled Trial." *JMIR Mental Health* 5 no. 4 (2018): e11290. doi:10.2196/11290.

Zaider, T. I., R. G. Heimberg, and M. Iida. "Anxiety Disorders and Intimate Relationships: A Study of Daily Processes in Couples." *Journal of Abnormal Psychology* 119 no. 1 (2010): 163–173. doi:10.1037/a0018473.

Index

About the Author

 **Sarah Belarde, LCSW,** has always had an interest in people and relationships. She received her master's in social work from the University of Southern California and has worked as a social worker and therapist for the last nine years. During this time she has worked in community and school mental health, hospital social work, and juvenile justice, and also as a private practice therapist. Most recently, she is focusing her work to collaborate with clients experiencing their own relationship anxiety and other anxieties. You can learn more about Sarah and her work as a therapist on her Instagram @sarahbelardetherapy.